FRAUD AND RESPONSIBILITY IN NONPROFIT ORGANIZATIONS

Strategies managers need to know about embezzlement by employees...

Dr. Marvin L. J. Blye

DBA-Accounting, Chief Executive Officer (CEO) of The Blye Group Maryland, USA

https://orcid.org/0000-0003-4029-0033

Email: marvinljblye@gmail.com

Dr. Desire Luamba

DBA-Finance, Vice President and CFO, Start Light Consulting LLC, Manassas, VA-USA

https://orcid.org/0000-0001-5138-1550

Email: luambade@gmail.com and Desire@gobrightstar.com

FRAUD AND RESPONSIBILITY **IN NONPROFIT ORGANIZATIONS**

From the Authors

Dear readers,

We wrote this book to help leaders, managers, researchers, students, and the public learn about fraud. The book provides useful information about fraud's nature, origin, and effects on nonprofit organizations.

The book also provides examples and case studies that help our readers better understand fraud and responsibility in nonprofit organizations. Fraud can have different implications, so it's important for nonprofit managers and leaders to manage and mitigate it in a timely manner. Mitigating fraud also contributes to improving trust among organizational stakeholders. We hope the examples and case studies presented in this book are helpful in determining the real causes and responsibility of fraud and how to prevent it in any nonprofit organization.

Our goal in writing this book is to give readers a big-picture view of fraud and its multiple implications. Additionally, the book examines the twin topics of fraud and the roles of managers in preventing it. This will build and maintain a positive image for the organization.

FRAUD AND RESPONSIBILITY **IN NONPROFIT ORGANIZATIONS**

Thank you for getting our book. We hope you enjoy it and find it helpful. Please feel free to reach out to us with any questions. **Link to the inspiration behind the book:**
https://www.proquest.com/openview/4394136837a59e806840f152df017871/1?pq-origsite=gscholar&cbl=44156

Dr. Marvin Blye   Dr. Desire Luamba

For more information about this book, scan the **QR Code**

FRAUD AND RESPONSIBILITY **IN NONPROFIT ORGANIZATIONS**

Authors' Commitment
Responsibility. Ability. Creativity

Dr. Marvin L. J. Blye

Dr. Marvin L. J. Blye is an accomplished and experienced Chief Fiscal Officer with many years of experience managing fiscal operations. His long experience lies in leading by promoting innovative strategies to increase transparency and implement accountability in fiscal operations. He advises senior leaders and managers to implement fiscal, accounting, and financial strategies to meet shareholder satisfaction.

Dr. Desire Luamba

Dr. Desire Luamba has worked in the business and financial industries for many years. His professional experience includes using financial and statistical tools to make long—and short-term accounting, budgeting, and financial decisions. He advises businesses on analyzing costs, accounting issues, business problems, and financial statements. He also conducts audit work and develops business model plans based on innovation and diversification strategies.

Acknowledgments

We sincerely thank everyone who supported us in writing and publishing this book.

The hard work that went into getting this book published could not have been done without the encouragement we received from all our colleagues, family members, and friends. Your positive contributions were instrumental in shaping it into a valuable resource for government leaders, business managers, researchers, students, and the general public.

We especially want to thank all the businesses and organizations that voluntarily agreed to share their case studies with us. These practical examples will help our readers better understand the nature, causes, and types of fraud and their implications for nonprofit organizations. These businesses and organizations provided us with what we are sure our readers will find to be valuable inspiration for understanding fraud and responsibility in their organizations.

We also wish to acknowledge the support of our editors, proofreaders, and book layout designers. We must not forget our loved ones (The Blye and Luamba families), who stood by us with unwavering encouragement and understanding throughout the making of this book. Your love and support were our constant motivation, driving us toward completing this project.

Last but not least, we acknowledge everyone else who contributed in some way to the completion of this book. We strove to make it a valuable resource for knowledge and management.

With our heartfelt gratitude,

Dr. Marvin L. J. Blye

Dr. Desire S. Luamba

Contents

Foreword   1

General Introduction   5

Section 1: The Nature, Causes, and Implications of Fraud in Nonprofit Organizations   7

Chapter 1. Nonprofit Organizations
- 1.1 Introduction   9
- 1.2 What is a Nonprofit Organization?   11
- 1.3 Types of Nonprofit Organizations   12
- 1.4 Chapter Summary   14
- 1.5 Case Study   16

Chapter 2. The Nature of Fraud
- 2.1 Introduction   21
- 2.2 What is "Fraud"?   22
- 2.3 Ethical Norms About Fraud   27
- 2.4 Fraud in the Workplace   30
- 2.5 Chapter Summary   33
- 2.6 Case Study   35

Chapter 3. Types of Fraud
- 3.1 Introduction   39
- 3.2 Fraud in Nonprofit Organizations   41
- 3.3 New Modern Types of Fraud   42
- 3.4 Chapter Summary   45
- 3.5 Case Study   47

Chapter 4. Implications of Fraud on the Organization

    4.1 Introduction   51
    4.2 Implications on Financial Asset   52
    4.3 Implications for Vendors   54
    4.4 Implications for Donors   56
    4.5 Implications for Government   57
    4.6 Implications for Employees   59
    4.7 Chapter Summary   61
    4.8 Case Study   64

Section 2: Responsibility   69

Chapter 5. Fraud Detection

    5.1 Introduction   77
    5.2 How to Detect Fraud?   78
    5.3 Who Detects Fraud?   81
    5.4 Why Detect Fraud?   84
    5.5 Where to Detect Fraud?   86
    5.6 When to Detect Fraud?   88
    5.7 Chapter Summary   91
    5.8 Case Study   94

Chapter 6. Prevention of Fraud in Nonprofit Organizations

    6.1 Introduction   99
    6.2 How to Prevent Fraud?   100
    6.3 Who Should Prevent Fraud?   103
    6.4 Why Preventing Fraud?   105
    6.5 Where to Prevent Fraud?   107
    6.6 Chapter Summary   110
    6.7 Case Study   113

Chapter 7. Challenges of Detecting and Preventing Fraud
    7.1 Introduction   117
    7.2 Challenges of Detecting Fraud   120
    7.3 Challenges of Preventing Fraud   123
    7.4 Chapter Summary   126
    7.5 Case Study   128

Chapter 8. Advantages of Detecting and Preventing Fraud in Nonprofit Organizations
    8.1 Introduction   131
    8.2 Advantages of Detecting Fraud in Nonprofit Organizations   133
    8.3 Advantages of Preventing Fraud in Nonprofit Organizations   136
    8.4 Chapter Summary   139
    8.5 Case Study   141

General Summary   **145**

Appendix A: Acronyms & Abbreviations

ARC- American Red Cross

CEO- Chief Executive Officer

CFO- Chief Financial Officer

DFM- Disposition-Based on Fraud Model

FER- Fundraising Efficiency Ratio

GAAP- Generally Accepted Accounting Principles

ISC- International Salvation Council

IT- Information Technology

NGO- Non-Governmental Organization

SEC- Securities and Exchange Commission

Foreword

If you were on a TV game show and the host was to say, "Top 8 answers on the board... we asked 100 people, 'Name a high-profile fraud?'" The answers might be FTX cryptocurrency, Enron, Bernie Madoff, Wells Fargo, Volkswagen, Lehman Brothers, etc. What do these have in common? Big dollars. Newsworthy. The stuff that sells newspapers and TV advertising.

The public might be lulled into a false perception that fraud seems to only occur in these big companies and that, if we don't hear about fraud in the news, it must not be occurring. That's akin to sticking our heads in the sand and hoping it won't happen to us.

Is that true? Do bad actors only target big corporations where there's lots of money? Unfortunately, no. Every organization of every size, in every industry, and in every country is susceptible to fraud. Yes, even in the not-for-profit sector. Charitable organizations, hospitals, local government, education, philanthropic groups, you name it, the risk of fraud exists. In these organizations, because of the razor-thin line of operating in the black, a fraud amount that might not be more than a blip on the radar for larger corporations could be catastrophic. Beyond the adverse financial impact of fraud is often the larger cost to nonprofit organizations – reputational damage.

In my over three decades of internal audit, compliance, and risk management leadership in the higher education sector, I have investigated dozens of frauds and examined internal controls in all parts of the organization. I've attended countless conference sessions, webinars, and workshops and read innumerable books and articles on fraud. Those materials are primarily aimed at higher-profile cases, as referenced in the game show question above. This requires those in the not-for-profit sector to translate the points to determine what applies to our industry.

If only there were a resource dedicated exclusively to covering the subject of fraud in the non-profit sector, one that would speak to the specific nuances in our domains. Enter Dr. Marvin L. J. Blye and Dr. Desire Luamba, two experienced accounting and finance experts and accomplished academicians. Their book, "Fraud and Responsibility in Nonprofit Organizations," is a must-read for nonprofit organization leaders.

Drs. Blye and Luamba have covered the subject thoroughly and methodically, from the nature and types of fraud to the implications when fraud occurs. They speak to effective practices and associate challenges in detecting and preventing fraud. Case studies are not shared in a salacious manner for entertainment's sake. Instead, they cite specific examples of fraud by dissecting the lessons learned so the reader emerges equipped with strategies they can implement. The authors cover the subject comprehensively and with academic rigor, giving the reader confidence that the principles are well-researched.

Who should read this book? The apparent audience would be auditors, compliance, and risk management professionals. To stop there, however, would be to feed into the misconception that exists in many organizations that internal control matters are the responsibility of the auditors and bean counters.
I strongly recommend that this be required reading for CEOs, CFOs, and all members of the C-Suite.
I would recommend this be in the library of every board member – especially members of the audit, finance, and legal committees. Why? A common thread in every fraud I have ever encountered over the years is the lack of visibility and monitoring of critical controls by the organization's senior leadership. The importance of promoting a culture of compliance and internal control in the tone at the top of the organization cannot be overstated.

In addition to the leadership, this book should be read by every manager, line-level supervisor, and every person who is expected to examine, approve, or process transactions as part of their job responsibilities.

If it sounds like I'm recommending that this be required reading for everyone at the organization, you're not far off. A dental hygienist friend of mine often quips to his patients, "Only floss the teeth that you want to keep." The same principle applies here. Only share this book with the people at your organization you want to help reduce the likelihood of fraud.

The subject is critical. This book is that important.
Robert Clark, Jr., CIA, CCEP, CBM, CVP
Chief Audit and Compliance Officer
Howard University
https://www.linkedin.com/in/robclarkjr/

General Introduction

Detecting and preventing fraud has become essential for promoting an organization's image, reputation, trust, and responsibility.[1] Implementing regular, periodic, and unscheduled audits or controls of an organization's activities could help improve the organization's performance.[2] An organization is a critical entity that managers can rely on to meet the company's goals and accomplish the organization's missions. In nonprofit organizations, managers implement strategies and manage daily, weekly, and monthly organizational activities to increase customers' and donors' satisfaction. As fraud may negatively affect the organization's performance, integrating the concepts of the fraud triangle could be significant in increasing transparency.[2] Fraud analysis could help organizations reduce their risk of becoming victims of fraud, protect customers from abuse, and help maintain their reputation.[3]

In addition, many nonprofit organizations fail to meet their missions because of scandals and fraudulent acts of their employees, managers, or leaders.[3] Skimming cash, purchasing schemes, and financial statement fraud are types of fraud that nonprofit managers should detect and prevent.[2] Some researchers argued that fraud arises from theft, investment fraud, embezzlement, and other unauthorized uses of funds.

---

[1] Blye, M. L. (2020). *Reducing the Frequency and Effects of Fraudulent Activities in Community Action Agencies* (Doctoral dissertation, Walden University).

[2] Blye, M. L., & Luamba, D. (2021). Fraud in nonprofit organizations: How to mitigate it. International Journal of Business and Management, 4, 385-392.

[3] Olaoye, G. O. (2024). Explainability and Interpretability in Fraud Detection Models.

So therefore, it is paramount to understand the concept of fraud and its impacts on organizational activities because fraud is a crime that may lead to losing millions of dollars and jobs in an organization.[1]

To conclude, managers in nonprofit organizations must perform services or goods to increase customers' satisfaction or donors' contribution to promote the business. As fraud negatively affects business performance, integrating the concepts of mitigating fraud could be a positive action to increase transparency in the operation activities. Finally, exploring and analyzing the impacts of fraud in nonprofit organizations could improve the relationship between managers, government agency leaders, and private or official contributors.[2]

This book equips leaders and organizations with critical tools to detect and prevent fraud, enhancing responsibility across nonprofit sectors.

---

[1] Olaoye, G. O. (2024). Explainability and Interpretability in Fraud Detection Models.

[2] Blye, M. L. (2020). *Reducing the Frequency and Effects of Fraudulent Activities in Community Action Agencies* (Doctoral dissertation, Walden University).

Section 1: The Nature, Causes, and Implications of Fraud in Nonprofit Organizations

Fraud within nonprofit organizations poses a complex challenge, intertwining financial mismanagement with ethical breaches and organizational vulnerabilities. While nonprofits are driven by altruistic missions to serve communities and advance social causes, they are not immune to fraudulent activities.[1] That's why understanding the multifaceted nature, underlying causes, and far-reaching implications of fraud in nonprofit organizations is essential for stakeholders to safeguard resources, uphold integrity, and sustain public trust. To be sure about the intricate dynamics surrounding fraud, this section delves into the factors contributing to fraud occurrence, the multifaced forms that it may take, and the profound consequences it can entail for the organization and the broader community that nonprofit organizations serve.

---

[1] Blye, M. L., & Luamba, D. (2021). Fraud in nonprofit organizations: How to mitigate it. International Journal of Business and Management, 4, 385-392.

Chapter 1

Nonprofit Organizations

1.1 Introduction

Nonprofit organizations play a vital role in society by addressing critical social, environmental, and cultural needs that government or for-profit organizations may not adequately accomplish. Nonprofits often serve as a safety net, providing essential services and support to vulnerable populations that may fall through the cracks of government programs or lack access to for-profit services.[1] Some nonprofits advocate for social change and policy reform. They amplify the voices of marginalized communities, advocate for human rights, and work to address systemic injustices.

Moreover, nonprofit organizations strengthen communities by fostering connections, promoting

---
[1] Luamba, D., Chagadama, J., Blye, M. L., James, K. C., & Jaman, S. H. (2023). Understanding the Factors of High Employee Turnover in Nonprofit Organizations: A Qualitative Case Study.

civic engagement, and building social capital. Nonprofit organizations unite people around common causes and encourage a sense of belonging and solidarity.

Nonprofits are often more flexible and innovative than government agencies or large corporations.[1] They can pilot new ideas, test innovative approaches, and adapt quickly to changing needs and circumstances. They also play a crucial role in preserving cultural diversity, advocating environmental protection and sustainability, and preserving natural habitats. Also, they promote conservation practices and raise awareness about environmental issues.

Additionally, volunteerism and civic engagement are also among nonprofits' missions, as they rely heavily on volunteers who donate their time, skills, and resources to support important causes.

In general, nonprofit organizations are essential pillars of civil society. To sum up, they address societal needs, promote social justice and equity, and promote positive social change in communities worldwide.

----

[1] Luamba, D., Chagadama, J., Blye, M. L., James, K. C., & Jaman, S. H. (2023). Understanding the Factors of High Employee Turnover in Nonprofit Organizations: A Qualitative Case Study.

1.2 What is a Nonprofit Organization?

A nonprofit organization operates with a fundamentally distinct purpose compared to a for-profit entity. A nonprofit organization does not focus on financial gain but on a deep commitment to societal betterment. Unlike profit-driven enterprises, a nonprofit organization's mission is to address social issues, foster positive change, and serve the community. Rather than pursuing financial profit, nonprofits aim to fulfill a specific societal need, such as advancing education, alleviating poverty, promoting environmental sustainability, or supporting health initiatives.[1] A nonprofit's success is to ensure a positive impact on the lives of individuals and the broader community. Nonprofit organizations should encourage collaboration, volunteerism, and partnerships with like-minded entities by emphasizing collective efforts to create lasting, meaningful change for the greater good.[2]

---

[1] Luamba, D. S., Chagadama, J., Blye, M. L., & James, K. C. (2022). The Impacts of Audit Transparency on Increasing Trust in Nonprofit Organizations. *Global Scientific and Academic Research Journal of Economics, Business, and Management*, 1(20), 86-96.

[2] Blye, M. L., & Luamba, D. (2021). Fraud in nonprofit organizations: How to mitigate it. *International Journal of Business and Management*, 4, 385-392.

1.3 Types of Nonprofit Organizations

Based on their mission, focus areas, and legal structure, there are different types of nonprofit organizations:

Charitable Organizations: These nonprofits primarily focus on providing direct services or support to those in need. They may include organizations that address poverty relief, healthcare access, education, and disaster relief.

Educational Institutions: Nonprofit educational institutions include schools, colleges, universities, and educational foundations. Their mission is to provide quality education and promote learning and intellectual growth.

Religious Organizations: These nonprofits are religious institutions that promote religious beliefs, practices, and community services. They may include churches, mosques, temples, and synagogues.

Arts and Culture Organizations: Nonprofits in this category promote and preserve artistic and cultural heritage. They may include museums, theaters, orchestras, dance companies, and cultural centers.

Environmental Organizations: These nonprofits focus on environmental conservation, sustainability, and advocacy. They work to protect natural habitats, promote conservation practices, and raise awareness about environmental issues.

Healthcare Organizations: Nonprofit organizations provide medical services, research, and advocacy to improve public health and well-being. They may include hospitals, clinics, research institutes, and public health organizations.

Social Advocacy Groups: These nonprofits advocate for social change, human rights, and social justice. They may address civil rights, gender equality, LGBTQ+ rights, and immigration reform.

Animal Welfare Organizations: Nonprofits in this category work to protect and promote the welfare of animals. They may include animal shelters, rescue organizations, wildlife conservation groups, and advocacy organizations.

Foundations: Foundations are nonprofits that provide funding and support to other charitable organizations or initiatives. They may focus on specific causes or issues and provide grants, scholarships, and other financial support.

Professional Associations: These nonprofits serve professionals in specific industries or fields by providing networking opportunities, professional development, and advocacy. They may include trade associations, professional societies, and industry-specific organizations.

These are just a few examples, and many other types of nonprofit organizations address a wide range of social, cultural, environmental, and humanitarian issues.

1.4 Chapter Summary

As explained above, nonprofit organizations play a crucial role in addressing societal needs and fostering positive change, operating with a societal mission-driven focus rather than making profits. By advocating for social change, building communities, and promoting environmental conservation, nonprofits contribute significantly to the well-being of individuals and the local community or society. It's essential to recognize that while nonprofit organizations complement the efforts of government agencies and for-profit entities, they also serve distinct functions by prioritizing social impact over financial gain. The role of the government in this context is to provide regulatory oversight, support through funding or partnerships, and create an enabling environment for nonprofits to thrive and fulfill their missions effectively. Together, nonprofits and government agencies can collaborate to address complex social challenges and build an equitable and sustainable future for all individuals in the local communities. This collaboration will help to build an equitable and sustainable future for all individuals in the local communities.

1.5 Case Study: Nonprofit Organization: International Salvation Council (ISC)

Introduction: The International Salvation Council (ISC) is a small NGO serving individuals and families in the Washington, D.C., metropolitan area. ISC's commitment to its mission and effective financial practices allow this organization to achieve its goals and positively impact the community.

Mission and Goals: ISC's mission is to provide essential services to those in need, regardless of their background, and to promote well-being and self-sufficiency. The organization's goals include providing interpretation, housing support, counseling services, and immigration and employment assistance to refugees and immigrants in the region [1].

Management Style: ISC strongly emphasizes control and reporting. The organization maintains a robust database that tracks client demographics, program utilization, and outcomes. This data-driven approach enables ISC to monitor its impact, identify trends, and make informed decisions.

Financial Sustainability and Stewardship: ISC's exemplary transparency managerial practices contribute significantly to its ability to fulfill its mission and achieve its goals.

---

[1] International Salvation Council (2022). *Our Mission and Vision.* Retrieved from https://intersalvationcouncil.org/

1. **Transparent Financial Reporting**: ISC maintains transparent and accurate financial reporting, providing stakeholders with a clear overview of the organization's financial health. Financial reports are shared with the board members, staff, donors, and the public.

2. **Diverse Revenue Streams**: The organization has established a diversified funding portfolio, including government grants, private donations, corporate partnerships, and fundraising events. This diversity reduces dependency on a single funding source, ensuring financial stability even in uncertain economic conditions.

3. **Strategic Budgeting**: ISC employs a strategic managing process that aligns with its mission and goals. Each program's budget is carefully developed, considering revenue and expenses, and reviewed regularly to ensure alignment with the organization's goals.

4. **Cost Efficiency**: The organization focuses on cost efficiency without compromising the quality of its services. This is achieved through carefully monitoring expenditures, negotiating vendor contracts, and seeking opportunities for shared resources.

5. **Reserve Fund and Financial Planning**: ISC maintains a reserve fund to buffer against

unexpected financial challenges. This prudent approach to financial planning demonstrates the organization's commitment to long-term sustainability.

6. **Internal Solid Controls:** ISC has implemented robust internal controls to prevent fraud and ensure the responsible use of funds. These include regular audits, separation of financial duties, and adherence to ethical accounting practices.

7. **Impact Measurement**: ISC quantifies its impact by tracking key performance indicators and outcomes. For example, in 2023, the organization served 67 families for quarter 1 (Q1) with food assistance and financial counseling. Satisfaction rate: 88%. For Q2, families served 60 with educational resources and job training. Satisfaction rate 90%. For Q3, families served 55 with food assistance and health workshops. Satisfaction rate 88%. For Q4, families served 70 with food assistance, housing support, and community events. Satisfaction rate 90%. Total families served 252 with an average satisfaction rate of 89%. The organization uses this data to showcase its effectiveness to stakeholders and make informed decisions about resource allocation

ISC's sound accounting and finance practices are pivotal in enabling the organization to meet its mission and goals effectively. Through transparent financial reporting, diversified revenue streams, strategic budgeting, and prudent financial planning, ISC has established itself as a model for financial management within the nonprofit sector. These practices ensure the organization's financial sustainability and contribute to its ability to create a positive and lasting impact on the community it serves. [1]

---

[1] International Salvation Council (2022). *Our Mission and Vision.* Retrieved from https://intersalvationcouncil.org/

Chapter 2

The Nature of Fraud

2.1 Introduction

Fraud within nonprofit organizations presents a complex challenge, as these entities often operate with missions centered on social welfare, humanitarian aid, or community development. Unlike for-profit businesses, nonprofits rely heavily on public trust and donations to fulfill their objectives, making any misuse of funds or misrepresentation particularly damaging. Fraud in nonprofits can take various forms that may be visible or invisible. Additionally, the inherent altruistic nature of nonprofits may create an environment where individuals are less likely to suspect fraudulent behavior, leading to vulnerabilities in oversight and accountability. Understanding the nature of fraud in nonprofit organizations is essential for implementing robust internal controls and maintaining the integrity necessary to fulfill their charitable missions effectively.

2.2 What is "Fraud"?

Doctor Donald Cressey, a criminologist, defined FRAUD as any deception acts to achieve a gain. Per Donald Cressey, people in organizations commit fraud for diverse reasons. The primary causes of fraud, as described by Donal Cressey, are opportunity, pressure, and rationalization. As shown in the figure below (fig 1). These three elements linked together allow individuals to commit fraud. Fraud is a significant business activity in the current business environment. Previous researchers noted that one of the most critical problems to the world's economy had been the lack of efficient organization controls and transparency. The lack of effective reporting and monitoring leads to corrupt behaviors surrounding cases such as corporate financial scandals.[1] Because of the complexity of the fraud phenomenon, some scholarly analysts have different views about fraud conception. Understanding the causes and effects of these unethical behaviors may significantly help nonprofit leaders when such acts occur to prevent it.

---

[1] Rafay, A. (Ed.). (2023). *Concepts, Cases, and Regulations in Financial Fraud and Corruption*. IGI Global.

Fig 1: Fraud Triangle Theory

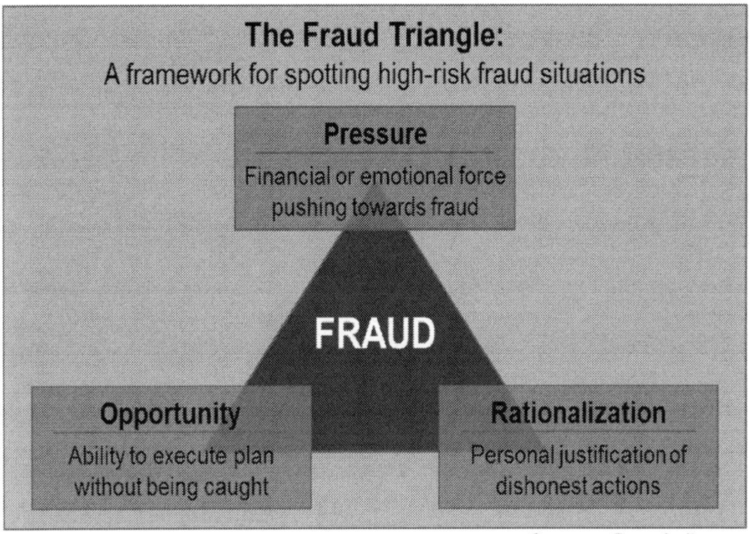

The Fraud Triangle:
A framework for spotting high-risk fraud situations

Pressure
Financial or emotional force pushing towards fraud

FRAUD

Opportunity
Ability to execute plan without being caught

Rationalization
Personal justification of dishonest actions

Source: Google Image

The fraud triangle theory, proposed by sociologist Donald Cressey, provides a framework for understanding the underlying factors that lead individuals to commit fraud. The Fraud Triangle hypothesizes that all three components, pressure, rationalization, and opportunity, coincide for fraud to happen. [1]

Per Cressey, fraud is an unethical or criminal act that negatively affects the entire community and organizations. Fraud should be seen as an unethical or criminal act that negatively affects the entire community and organizations.

Acknowledging that individuals can commit fraud at any time and in any organization is essential. Nonprofit leaders should analyze and fully understand the causes of their employees' financial

---
[1] Cressey's (1953). Other people's money: A study in the social psychology of embezzlement. New York, NY, US: Free Press.

fraud and find strategies to mitigate fraud for organizational performance. The indications of fraudulent activities may result in a short or long-term lack of liquidity or customer deception.

Pressure

Individual pressure is an influence on individuals to engage in fraudulent activities, which can cause financial problems for the organization. Pressure is the motivation that leads to acting unethically. Most individuals require some form of pressure to commit a criminal act, and every fraud perpetrator faces some burden to commit unethical behavior for many reasons. Ethical knowledge is important to moderate the relationship between pressure and organizational fraud because ethics, directly and indirectly, influence work engagement and organizational misbehavior.[1]

In a problematic situation, fraud arises where there is a chance to commit it without a high chance of prosecution. Financial pressure, such as the inability to pay bills, the desire to buy expensive cars, or provide basic needs for family members, are motivators of the pressure of committing fraud. Non-financial pressures associated with gambling and drug addiction are also factors that lead individuals to engage in unethical behaviors. Business managers or leaders must implement ethical values and strategies to help employees see fraud as negative behavior or revenge against their employers.

---

[1] Blye, M. L. (2020). *Reducing the Frequency and Effects of Fraudulent Activities in Community Action Agencies* (Doctoral dissertation, Walden University).

Moreover, non-shareable financial pressures are financial stresses that an employee can experience in an organization. Also, workers' dissatisfaction and perceived inequities are the main predictors that motivate and contribute to work-related non-sharable financial pressures and fraudulent acts in the workplace. Individuals might commit fraud because of non-sharable financial pressure. Nonprofit leaders have the role of learning and understanding the nature of non-financial pressure their employees may face to mitigate the effects of fraudulent acts.

Opportunity

Opportunity represents the conditions enabling individuals to commit fraudulent acts without detection. It includes weak internal controls, lack of oversight, and access to resources without adequate supervision. When there's a perceived gap in monitoring or enforcement within an organization, individuals may seize the opportunity to exploit these vulnerabilities for personal gain. The opportunity to engage in fraud increases as the organization's control structure weakens. This opportunity also happens when corporate governance becomes less effective and the quality of its audit functions deteriorates. Similarly, the opportunity for an individual or group of individuals to commit fraud is often due to the company's lack of supervision or regular internal controls. The lack of internal controls promotes an atmosphere that may motivate, create, or present an opportunity to commit a crime.[1] When internal controls are weak or if there is a lack of ineffective board governance, opportunities to commit fraudulent acts increase.[1] Also, if someone in a position of trust violates that trust to address non-sharable financial pressures, the perceived opportunity to commit fraud arises. Based on the fraud triangle theory, despite the pressure an individual may or may not face, the risk of committing financial fraud is always permanent unless there is no opportunity.

Rationalization

Rationalization is the third element of the fraud triangle and refers to the mental process through which individuals justify their fraudulent actions to themselves. They may convince themselves that their behavior is acceptable or necessary given their circumstances, thereby mitigating feelings of guilt or moral conflict. Rationalization increases the likelihood of a person committing an unethical act or fraud. This is because individuals rationalize their behaviors and actions that support and justify their committing fraud.[1] As the third element of the fraud triangle, rationalization indicates that the fraud perpetrator must formulate morally acceptable ideas before engaging in unethical behavior. If an individual cannot justify dishonest actions, it is unlikely that they

---

[1] Yadiati, W., & Rezwiandhari, A. (2023). Detecting Fraudulent Financial Reporting In State-Owned Company: Hexagon Theory Approach. JAK (Jurnal Akuntansi) Kajian Ilmiah Akuntansi, 10(1), 128-147.

will engage in fraud. Policies and statements of ethics must be present in any organization to ensure success because it is always probable that individuals engage in fraud for diverse reasons. Nonprofit leaders are responsible for incorporating governing strategies in organizations that mitigate the rationalization of individuals from committing fraud.

2.3 Ethical Norms About Fraud

Ethical norms regarding fraud in organizations serve as guiding principles that dictate acceptable behavior and conduct regarding fraudulent activities. These norms are founded on principles of honesty, integrity, and accountability. They emphasize the importance of ethical decision-making at all levels of an organization. One fundamental ethical norm is prohibiting fraudulent behavior, encompassing activities such as embezzlement, falsifying financial records, and misrepresenting information. Organization managers or leaders must uphold high moral standards and maintain a zero-tolerance policy towards fraud, fostering a culture of transparency and trust among employees and stakeholders.

Moreover, ethical norms regarding fraud also entail reporting suspected fraudulent activities promptly. Employees have a moral responsibility to raise concerns and report any instances of alleged fraud to appropriate authorities. To do so, they have to use internal channels established for whistleblowing. Organizations can effectively deter fraudulent behavior and safeguard their integrity and reputation by promoting a culture of accountability and encouraging open communication.[1] Upholding ethical norms regarding fraud ensures compliance with legal and regulatory requirements and fosters a culture of integrity and moral conduct, contributing to long-term success and sustainability.[2]

Additionally, Fraud may not always be visible and accessible to detect in nonprofit organizations. Sometimes, leaders may have to increase internal controls or promote ethical values to mitigate fraud. Individuals aware of decisions and behaviors to commit fraud make a moral decision. People can commit fraud using nonfamiliar sources such as the internet, textbooks, journal articles, etc. This happens because nonfamiliar sources are the main cause of a lack of ethical values consisting of an organization's principles, policies, and guidelines for good governance and management operations. To understand fraud's nature, organizational managers in nonprofit organizations should promote ethical values and establish credible layers of code of conduct that may detect and prevent fraudulent practices.[1]

---
[1] Blye, M. L., & Luamba, D. (2021). Fraud in nonprofit organizations: How to mitigate it. International Journal of Business and Management, 4, 385-392.
[2] Luamba, D., Chagadama, J., Blye, M. L., James, K. C., & Jaman, S. (2023). Understanding the Factors of High Employee Turnover in Nonprofit Organizations: A Qualitative Case Study

Furthermore, the ethical theory leads to certain qualities that define appropriate behavior and the right action to undertake for the organization's benefit. People acting and making decisions within an organization have the power and authority structures to implement ethical norms. Promoting ethical values should concern everyone at all organizational levels because high leaders or top managers can also commit fraud. As explained above, the three primary perceptions influencing individuals' choices to engage in fraud are pressure, opportunity, and rationalization.

For example, if a manager adheres to ethical or moral standards, his attitude and position may influence followers to comply with ethical values and contribute to detecting and mitigating fraud. Leaders must increasingly monitor compliance with ethical codes and standards to promote trust and discourage fraud. However, poor management monitoring controls may lead to weaknesses in ethical and moral values and fraud detection. The fundamental tenets of ethical theory are critical for nonprofit organization managers to provide strategies to mitigate fraud and increase stakeholder confidence.

---

[1] Blye, M. L., & Luamba, D. (2021). Fraud in nonprofit organizations: How to mitigate it. International Journal of Business and Management, 4, 385-392.

2.4 Fraud in the Workplace

Fraud in the workplace poses a significant threat to nonprofit organizations, potentially undermining their financial stability and tarnishing their reputations. Fraudulent activities can have far-reaching consequences, whether through embezzlement, falsifying financial records, or other deceptive practices. Beyond the immediate financial losses, fraud can erode trust among employees and stakeholders, leading to a breakdown in morale and productivity. Moreover, discovering fraud can result in legal consequences, damaging lawsuits, and regulatory penalties, further exacerbating the organization's challenges.[1]

Also, corruption or a lack of effective control mechanisms within an organization can create an environment ripe for fraudulent behavior to thrive. Employees who perceive a culture of impunity or lax oversight may be more inclined to engage in unethical conduct for personal gain. Additionally, the absence of clear policies and procedures for detecting and reporting fraud can further embolden dishonest individuals to exploit vulnerabilities within the system. As a result, organizations must prioritize implementing robust internal controls, fostering a culture of integrity, and promoting transparency to deter fraudulent activities effectively.

---

[1] Blye, M. L. (2020). *Reducing the Frequency and Effects of Fraudulent Activities in Community Action Agencies* (Doctoral dissertation, Walden University

Furthermore, leadership is crucial in combating fraud and fostering an ethical work environment. Organizational managers must lead by example, demonstrating a steadfast commitment to ethical conduct and accountability. By setting clear expectations and standards of behavior, managers can help cultivate a culture where fraud is unacceptable and swiftly addressed. For instance, proactive measures such as regular audits, segregation of duties, and whistleblower protection programs can empower employees to identify and report fraudulent activities without retaliation.[1] Additionally, mitigating the risk of fraud requires a multifaceted approach that combines managerial tools with ongoing education and training initiatives. Managers should invest in continuous learning opportunities to ensure employees have the knowledge and skills to recognize and prevent fraudulent behavior.[1] Therefore, fostering open communication channels where employees feel comfortable raising concerns or suspicions is essential for early detection and intervention of fraud.

---

[1] Blye, M. L., & Luamba, D. (2021). Fraud in nonprofit organizations: How to mitigate it. *International Journal of Business and Management*, 4, 385-392.

Then, mitigating the risk of fraud requires a multifaceted approach that combines managerial tools with ongoing education and training initiatives. Managers should invest in continuous learning opportunities to ensure employees have the knowledge and skills to recognize and prevent fraudulent behavior.[1] Additionally, fostering open communication channels where employees feel comfortable raising concerns or suspicions is essential for early detection and intervention. By fostering a culture of vigilance and accountability, organizations can safeguard their assets, uphold their integrity, and maintain the trust of their stakeholders in both profit and nonprofit sectors.[2]

Finally, fraud is a reality in workplaces, and employees can be the most significant source or cause of fraud. In the workplace human desires, intentions, and negative actions may occur at any time. Negative behavior, such as corruption, is an essential factor that can demotivate employees to reach a company's goals when it becomes routine. Based on the fraud triangle theory, nonprofit leaders should rely on the Disposition-Based on Fraud Model (DFM) to predict intentional fraud actions.

---

[1] Blye, M. L. (2020). *Reducing the Frequency and Effects of Fraudulent Activities in Community Action Agencies* (Doctoral dissertation, Walden University).

[2] Blye, M. L., & Luamba, D. (2021). Fraud in nonprofit organizations: How to mitigate it. *International Journal of Business and Management*, 4, 385-392.

2.5 Chapter Summary

At its core, fraud embodies deceitful actions undertaken to benefit oneself while inflicting harm on others. It encompasses a broad spectrum of deceptive behaviors, including financial manipulation, misrepresentation of facts, or exploitation of trust. Norms surrounding fraud are deeply rooted in societal and professional ethics, emphasizing principles such as honesty, integrity, and accountability. Violations of these norms not only erode trust but also carry severe consequences, including financial losses, damaged reputations, and legal repercussions.

In the context of the workplace, fraud presents a significant challenge to organizational stability and ethical integrity. Employers must implement robust internal controls and foster a culture of transparency to prevent and detect fraudulent activities. This entails establishing clear policies, conducting regular audits, and providing avenues for employees to report suspected misconduct without fear of retaliation. Despite these efforts, fraud in the workplace persists, often fueled by factors such as pressure to meet financial targets, insufficient oversight, or gaps in employee training on ethical standards.

Addressing fraud in the workplace requires a comprehensive approach that combines preventive measures with swift and decisive action against perpetrators. By promoting ethical behavior, reinforcing accountability, and prioritizing transparency, organizations can mitigate the risk of fraud and uphold the values of integrity and trust in professional environments.

2.6 Unveiling Fraud: A Case Study in a Nonprofit Organization

Introduction: Nonprofit organizations are built on principles of transparency, integrity, and altruism, making them crucial pillars of societal welfare. However, even within these noble endeavors, the specter of fraud can loom, undermining the foundations upon which these organizations stand. This case study delves into an instance of fraud within a nonprofit organization, examining its nature, the prevailing norms around fraud, and the impact of such misconduct in the workplace.

Case Study: The Harmony Foundation, a nonprofit dedicated to providing educational opportunities to underprivileged children, was lauded for its noble mission and tireless efforts.[1] However, behind the façade of goodwill, a fraud scheme was unfolding. The organization's finance manager, Steven Mark, had been siphoning funds for educational programs into his accounts for three years. Mark failed to report more than $1 million on federal tax returns and pretended that the money he earned came from the charitable foundation Harmony and Happiness. With clever manipulation of financial records and exploitation of trust, Mark managed to conceal his

---

[1] Harmony Education Foundation. (2023). About HEF. Retrieved from https://www.harmonyed.org/about/about-hef.

fraudulent activities, evading detection even during routine audits.

As norms surrounding fraud dictate, employees of the Harmony Foundation were expected to adhere to the highest ethical standards, with transparency and accountability being paramount.[1] However, a culture of unquestioning trust and insufficient oversight created fertile ground for fraudulent behavior to flourish. The prevailing belief in the inherent goodness of individuals within the organization, coupled with limited scrutiny of financial transactions, allowed the manager to exploit vulnerabilities and perpetrate his deceitful actions with impunity.

The revelation of fraud within the Harmony Foundation sent shockwaves through the organization, shattering the trust of donors, volunteers, and beneficiaries alike. Beyond the financial losses incurred, the incident tarnished the organization's reputation and cast doubts about its ability to fulfill its mission effectively. The aftermath necessitated a comprehensive reassessment of internal controls, including the implementation of stricter oversight mechanisms and enhanced transparency measures. Additionally, it underscored the importance of fostering a culture of vigilance, where employees are encouraged to raise concerns and report suspicious activities without fear of reprisal.

---

[1] Harmony Education Foundation. (2023). About HEF. Retrieved from https://www.harmonyed.org/about/about-hef.

Conclusion: The Harmony Foundation fraud case serves as a cautionary tale for nonprofit organizations, highlighting the critical importance of vigilance, transparency, and accountability in safeguarding against misconduct. By upholding ethical norms, strengthening internal controls, and promoting a culture of integrity, nonprofits can mitigate the risk of fraud and uphold the trust of stakeholders, ensuring their continued impact in advancing social welfare.

Chapter 3
Types of Fraud

3.1 Introduction

Fraud is a pervasive threat that transcends organizational boundaries, impacting nonprofit or for-profit organizations.. Within nonprofit organizations, which often operate with altruistic missions to serve communities and advance social causes, fraudulent activities can undermine the essence of their purpose. This may involve misappropriating funds for charitable initiatives, manipulating financial records to mislead donors and stakeholders, or exploiting trust among volunteers and staff. In contrast, for-profit organizations, driven by profit maximization, face different fraud risks that generally arise from fraudulent behaviors such as embezzlement, financial statement fraud, or unlawfully enriching for personal gain. Despite the differing motivations and operational objectives between nonprofit and for-profit organizations, the fundamental nature of fraud remains consistent. It involves intentional deception to achieve illicit ends, resulting in financial harm and erosion of trust.

Navigating the complexities of fraud in nonprofit and for-profit organizations and understanding each sector's unique challenges and vulnerabilities remains paramount. Then, navigating the complexities of fraud in nonprofit and for-profit organizations and understanding each sector's unique challenges and vulnerabilities remains paramount. Nonprofit organizations may face issues of transparency and oversight, while for-profits may face pressures to meet financial targets and regulatory compliance. Nevertheless, both sectors share a common imperative to uphold ethical standards, cultivate cultures of integrity, and implement robust internal controls to deter and detect fraudulent activities. By recognizing the multifaceted nature of fraud and adopting proactive measures to mitigate its risks, organizations can safeguard their reputation, preserve stakeholder trust, and fulfill their missions with integrity and accountability.

3.2 Fraud in Nonprofit Organizations

The causes and consequences of fraud in profit organizations are tremendous. However, fraud within nonprofit organizations presents unique challenges due to the often-limited resources and emphasis on serving the community rather than maximizing profits. Despite their altruistic missions, nonprofits are not immune to fraudulent activities, which can manifest in various forms, such as misappropriation of funds, fraudulent grant applications, or conflicts of interest among board members and executives[1].

Unlike for-profit entities, where financial gain may be the primary motive, fraud in nonprofits can stem from a combination of factors, including inadequate internal controls, lack of oversight, and individuals exploiting their positions for personal benefit.

One common avenue for fraud in nonprofits is through financial mismanagement, where funds intended for charitable purposes are diverted for personal use or non-mission-related expenses.

This misallocation of resources undermines the organization's ability to fulfill its mission and erodes the trust of donors and beneficiaries. Moreover, the complex nature of nonprofit accounting and reporting can provide opportunities for manipulation and concealment of fraudulent activities, making detection more challenging.

---

[1] Miller, S. (2022). *Strategies and Internal Control Procedures for Decreasing Fraud in Faith-Based Nonprofit Organizations.* Liberty University.

Another prevalent form of fraud in nonprofits involves conflicts of interest, where board members, executives, or employees exploit their positions for personal gain or advantage. This can include awarding contracts to affiliated businesses at inflated prices, steering donations toward personal interests, or using nonprofit resources for personal expenses. Such conflicts compromise the organization's integrity and raise ethical concerns and legal liabilities.

To mitigate these risks, nonprofits must implement robust governance structures, establish clear conflict-of-interest policies, and foster a culture of transparency and accountability at all levels of the organization.

3.3. New Modern Types of Fraud

In nonprofit organizations, fraud can take on various forms, including instances of Artificial Intelligence (AI) misuse, technological exploitation, theft, and misreporting. For instance, AI misuse may occur when nonprofits utilize AI-powered donation processing systems manipulated to siphon funds into unauthorized accounts or generate false donation records. This may happen, for example, when altering AI Parameters in the organization management system; it may help the hacker alter the AI parameters that validate donation transactions, making it easier to approve transactions from unauthorized accounts. Such fraudulent activities can deceive donors and mislead stakeholders about the true impact of their contributions, eroding trust and tarnishing the organization's reputation.

In addition, technological exploitation in nonprofits may involve the misuse of online fundraising platforms or crowdfunding websites. For instance, fraudsters may create fake campaigns or manipulate legitimate ones to solicit donations under pretenses. They might use deceptive tactics such as fabricating stories of hardship or misrepresenting the intended use of funds to elicit sympathy and maximize donations. Furthermore, cybercriminals may exploit vulnerabilities in the organization's IT infrastructure to gain unauthorized access to sensitive donor information or financial records, leading to data breaches and financial losses.

Fig 2. Fraud Practice

Source: Google Images

Theft within nonprofit organizations can occur in various ways, including embezzlement, petty cash pilferage, or asset misappropriation. Employees entrusted with handling cash donations or managing organizational funds may engage in embezzlement by diverting money for personal use or by falsifying financial records to cover their tracks. Moreover, theft of physical assets such as office supplies, equipment, or inventory can occur when proper controls and oversight mechanisms are lacking. Such incidents deplete the organization's resources and undermine its ability to fulfill its mission and serve its beneficiaries effectively.

Misreporting and fraudulent language are additional tactics used in nonprofit fraud schemes to deceive stakeholders and regulatory bodies. This may involve inflating program outcomes, exaggerating the impact of initiatives, or manipulating financial statements to conceal financial irregularities. Nonprofits may also engage in deceptive practices in their communication materials, using misleading language or imagery to solicit donations or secure funding.

These fraudulent activities not only distort the organization's true performance but also compromise its credibility and legitimacy within the philanthropic community. To combat fraud effectively, it is crucial for you, as a nonprofit executive, financial officer, or staff member responsible for financial management and governance, to implement stringent internal controls, conduct regular audits, and prioritize transparency and accountability in your operations and communications.

3.4 Chapter Summary

Fraud in both profit and nonprofit organizations encompasses a range of deceptive practices that individuals may employ to unlawfully gain personal advantage or manipulate organizational resources. In profit organizations, common forms of fraud include financial statement manipulation, embezzlement, insider trading, and procurement fraud. These activities often stem from the pressure to meet financial targets, the desire for personal gain, or the exploitation of weak internal controls. However, fraud can be particularly damaging in nonprofit organizations, where relationships with donors, beneficiaries, and stakeholders are built on trust and altruism. Nonprofits may fall victim to fraudulent activities such as misappropriating funds, falsifying financial records, deceptive fundraising practices, and technological exploitation. Given the inherent reliance on goodwill and transparency, fraud in nonprofit organizations erodes trust and undermines the organization's mission and credibility within the philanthropic community. Fraud in nonprofits requires robust internal controls, ethical leadership, and a commitment to accountability and transparency to safeguard the organization's integrity and maintain stakeholder trust.

3.5 Case Study: Fraudulent Activities in the American Red Cross

Background: The American Red Cross (ARC) is one of the largest and most well-known humanitarian organizations in the world, dedicated to alleviating human suffering, protecting life and health, uphold human dignity during armed conflicts and other emergencies. ARC was committed to assisting people affected by the aftermath of the 7.0 earthquake in Haiti 2010. The earthquake caused widespread destruction, leaving millions of people homeless and in desperate need of assistance. ARC launched a major fundraising campaign and raised over $500 million in donations from generous individuals and corporations. However, after an internal audit and control, ARC was embroiled in a scandal involving fraudulent activities perpetrated by several employees. This compromised the organization's integrity and betrayed its stakeholders' trust.[1]

Fraudulent Activities: The audit and control revealed multiple instances of employees misusing funds and housing materials for personal gain. Firstly, several staff members were found to have misappropriated funds allocated for program expenses by submitting falsified receipts and invoices for fictitious purchases. Investigations found that the ARC had contracted with companies for supplies and services at inflated prices. For instance, it was

[1] American Red Cross. (2010). *Haiti Earthquake*. Retrieved from https://www.redcross.org//dam/redcross/atg/PDF_s/HaitiEarthquake_OneYearReport.pdf.

reported that the cost of temporary shelters was significantly higher than similar projects managed by other organizations, leading to allegations that the funds were not being used efficiently. Additionally, employees abused their power and lack of control by pilfering medications, tents, and other housing materials for personal use or resale. These actions deprived the intended beneficiaries of essential resources and undermined the organization's ability to fulfill its mission effectively.

Moreover, a significant portion of the fraudulent activities centered around false reporting of the number of local employees and salaries. The ARC claimed to have built around 15,000 homes, but subsequent investigations revealed that many were incomplete or poorly constructed. Reports suggested that the number of quality homes built was much lower, raising concerns about the accuracy of their impact reporting. This scandal not only defrauded the organization of financial resources but also distorted records of program activities and volunteer contributions. As a result, the true impact of the organization's efforts was misrepresented, eroding trust among donors, partners, and the communities served.

Consequences and Response: The discovery of fraudulent activities within ARC profoundly affected its operations, reputation, and stakeholder relationships. Apart from the financial losses incurred, the organization faced public scrutiny, legal liabilities, and a loss of credibility within the philanthropic community. In response, the board of directors initiated comprehensive measures to address fraud, including disciplinary actions against implicated employees, strengthening internal controls and oversight mechanisms, and implementing rigorous monitoring and reporting procedures.

Moving forward, ARC was committed to rebuilding trust and transparency by prioritizing ethical conduct, accountability, and integrity in all its operations. The organization pledged to strengthen its governance structures, enhance staff training on ethical standards and compliance, and foster a culture of openness and responsibility. By learning from this unfortunate incident and implementing proactive measures to prevent future fraud, ARC aimed to regain the confidence of its stakeholders and reaffirm its commitment to serving its mission with integrity and sincerity.

Chapter 4

Implications of Fraud on the Organization

4.1 Introduction

Fraud can have far-reaching implications that extend beyond immediate financial losses. First, it damages the trust and confidence of stakeholders, including donors, beneficiaries, employees, and the broader community. Second, it erodes individuals' or organizations' faith in integrity and reliability, leading to strained relationships and diminished support. Lastly, fraud in nonprofit organizations devastates and jeopardizes the organization's ability to fulfill its mission and secure vital funding.

Furthermore, fraud can result in significant legal and reputational repercussions for the implicated individuals or organizations.

Legal consequences may include civil lawsuits, regulatory sanctions, fines, and criminal prosecution. Reputational damage, conversely, can tarnish the organization's standing within its industry or community. This situation would make attracting donors, partners, and talented staff challenging. Moreover, the negative publicity surrounding fraud can linger long after the incident, hindering the organization's ability to rebuild trust and restore its reputation. Thus, the implications of fraud go beyond financial loss, impacting the credibility, viability, and sustainability of the affected entity.[1]

4.2 Implications on Financial Asset

Fraud can have profound implications on nonprofit organizations' financial assets and jeopardize their ability to serve their intended beneficiaries effectively. For instance, financial fraud can lead to direct monetary losses through misappropriation of funds, embezzlement, or fraudulent financial transactions.[2] These losses deplete the organization's resources, limiting its capacity to invest in programs, services, and infrastructure for achieving its objectives. As a result, vital initiatives may be scaled back or

---

[1] Hamed, R. (2023). The role of internal control systems in ensuring financial performance sustainability. *Sustainability, 15*(13), 10206.
[2] Blye, M. L. (2020). *Reducing the Frequency and Effects of Fraudulent Activities in Community Action Agencies* (Doctoral dissertation, Walden University).

discontinued, depriving vulnerable communities of much-needed support and assistance.

Moreover, the discovery of financial fraud can erode the trust and confidence of donors and funding partners Losing faith and confidence can lead to contributors declining contributions and support. Donors expect their contributions to be used responsibly and ethically to advance the organization's mission and make a positive impact. However, instances of fraud undermine this trust, casting doubt on the organization's credibility and stewardship of resources. Consequently, donors may withdraw their support, redirect funding to other organizations, or hesitate to make future contributions, exacerbating the organization's financial challenges.

Additionally, the fallout from financial fraud can extend beyond immediate monetary losses, including legal fees, regulatory penalties, and increased insurance premiums. Nonprofit organizations may incur significant expenses in investigating and rectifying fraudulent activities and defending against potential lawsuits or regulatory actions. Furthermore, reputational damage resulting from the fraud can impact the organization's ability to secure grants, partnerships, and contracts. This may further constrain financial resources and impede nonprofit organizations' ability to achieve their missions. Thus, the implications of fraud on nonprofit organizational financial assets have multiple faces, affecting the bottom line and the organization's reputation, sustainability, and ability to make a difference in the community.

4.3 Implications for Vendors

Fraud within nonprofit organizations can have significant implications for their vendors and suppliers. For instance, vendors may suffer financial losses if they are victims of fraudulent activities such as false invoicing, fictitious purchases, or non-payment of goods or services rendered. Also, if fraudulent procurement practices are used by inflating invoices or fabricating purchase orders, vendors may find themselves providing goods or services without fair compensation. This undermines the trust and integrity of the business relationship and imposes financial hardships on the vendors, particularly small businesses or independent contractors reliant on timely payments.

Furthermore, fraud within nonprofit organizations can damage the reputation and credibility of their vendors. For example, if vendors unknowingly become associated with fraudulent activities perpetrated by nonprofit organizations, their integrity and trustworthiness may be questioned by other clients, partners, or stakeholders. Also, the negative publicity surrounding the fraud may tarnish the vendors' brand image, leading to a loss of business opportunities and customer confidence. Moreover, vendors may face legal and regulatory scrutiny if they are implicated in the fraudulent activities of nonprofit organizations, potentially resulting in fines, penalties, or damage to their professional reputation.

Additionally, fraud within nonprofit organizations can strain the vendor relationship, lead to strained communication, delay payments, and increase scrutiny of transactions. Vendors may become more cautious when dealing with the nonprofit. They may implement stricter payment terms or demand additional documentation to verify the legitimacy of transactions. This can create inefficiencies in the procurement process, increase administrative burden, and hinder collaboration between the nonprofit and its vendors. Ultimately, the implications of fraud on nonprofit organizational vendors extend beyond financial losses. They may include reputational damage, legal risks, and strained business relationships, highlighting the importance of ethical conduct and transparency in all business dealings.

4.4 Implications for Donors

The implications of fraud on donors in nonprofit organizations are multifaceted and can have significant consequences for the donors and the organizations they support. For instance, when donors discover fraudulent activities such as misuse or misappropriation of funds, it erodes their trust and confidence in the organization. Donors expect their contributions to be used responsibly and ethically to advance the nonprofit's mission and positively impact the community. However, instances of fraud can lead donors to question the integrity and effectiveness of the organization, causing them to reconsider their support and potentially redirect their contributions to other causes or organizations they perceive as more trustworthy.

Moreover, fraud can have financial implications for donors, particularly if they give significant monetary contributions or pledge long-term support to the nonprofit. Donors feel disillusioned and frustrated if they know their generosity or donations are misused or diverted. This can lead to feelings of betrayal and resentment as donors realize that their contributions did not have the intended impact they had hoped for. Furthermore, donors may incur additional costs or legal fees if they pursue legal action or seek restitution for their losses, further exacerbating the financial ramifications of fraud.

Additionally, reputational damage from fraud can tarnish the nonprofit's image and reflect poorly on its donors, particularly if they are publicly associated with the organization. Donors may face criticism or scrutiny from their peers, colleagues, or the media for their association with a nonprofit embroiled in scandal or controversy. This can damage their personal or professional reputation and undermine their credibility as philanthropists or advocates for social change. Consequently, the implications of fraud on donors in nonprofit organizations extend beyond financial losses. These implications also include emotional distress, reputational damage, and a loss of trust in the charitable sector.

4.5 Implications for the Government

Fraud within an organization can have significant implications for the government, particularly in cases involving nonprofit entities that receive government funding or tax-exempt status. Firstly, fraud can result in misappropriation or misuse of government funds for public welfare or social programs. When nonprofit organizations engage in fraudulent activities such as embezzlement, falsifying financial records, or misreporting of program outcomes, it undermines the government's trust and confidence in its ability to steward public resources effectively. This mismanagement of funds can lead to financial losses for the government and hinder its efforts to address pressing social issues or deliver essential services to citizens.[1]

Moreover, fraud within nonprofit organizations can damage the government's reputation and credibility, particularly if it is perceived as lax oversight or inadequate regulation. Instances of fraud may raise questions about the government's oversight mechanisms, accountability frameworks, and due diligence processes in vetting and monitoring nonprofit organizations. This can erode public trust in government institutions and undermine citizens' confidence in the integrity of the regulatory framework governing nonprofits.

Furthermore, the negative publicity surrounding fraud cases may fuel public skepticism about the government's ability to address fraud effectively and hold those responsible for wrongdoing accountable.

Additionally, fraud within nonprofit organizations can lead to increased regulatory scrutiny and enforcement actions by government agencies.

In response to fraud or financial mismanagement, government regulators may initiate investigations, audits, or compliance reviews. These actions are useful to assess the organization's adherence to legal and regulatory requirements. Also, this can impose additional administrative burdens and compliance

---

[1] Luamba, D. (2019). Strategies small business owners use to remain sustainable (Doctoral dissertation, Walden University).

costs on the nonprofit organization and the government. Furthermore, regulatory interventions such as revocation of tax-exempt status, suspension of government funding, or imposition of fines and penalties can seriously affect the organization's operations and sustainability. Thus, the implications of fraud in organizations for the government extend beyond financial losses. These implications may also include reputational damage, regulatory challenges, and erosion of public trust in the nonprofit sector.

4.6 Implications for Employees

The implications of fraud for nonprofit organization employees can be profound and wide-ranging. They may affect both the individuals directly involved in fraudulent activities and the broader workforce. Firstly, employees implicated in fraud may face severe disciplinary actions, including termination of employment, legal proceedings, and criminal charges. Secondly, apart from the immediate loss of jobs and income, individuals found guilty of fraudulent behavior may suffer long-term damage to their professional reputation. This situation may make it challenging to secure future employment opportunities within the nonprofit sector or elsewhere. Lastly, the stigma associated with being associated with fraud can have personal and psychological repercussions, leading to feelings of shame, guilt, and social isolation.

Furthermore, fraud within a nonprofit organization can erode trust and morale among the entire workforce, creating a toxic work environment characterized by suspicion, resentment, and disillusionment. Employees not involved in fraudulent activities may feel betrayed by their colleagues or superiors, leading to a breakdown in team cohesion and collaboration. Moreover, the discovery of fraud may raise questions about the organization's leadership, governance, and ethical standards, causing employees to question their commitment to its mission and values. This loss of trust and confidence can harm employee engagement, job satisfaction, and productivity, ultimately hindering the organization's ability to achieve its objectives and serve its beneficiaries effectively. [1]

Additionally, fraud within a nonprofit organization may trigger increased scrutiny and oversight by regulatory agencies, auditors, and donors. This may also place additional pressure on employees to comply with stringent reporting requirements and internal controls.

This can create a culture of fear and anxiety, where employees feel compelled to adhere to rigid protocols and procedures to avoid potential repercussions.

---

[1] Chagadama, J. (2022). Small construction business owners' strategies to reduce voluntary employee turnover (Doctoral dissertation, Walden University).

Moreover, the negative publicity surrounding fraud cases may tarnish the organization's reputation, making it difficult for employees to attract top talent or secure funding for critical programs and initiatives. The implications of fraud for nonprofit organization employees encompasses legal, financial, emotional, and reputational consequences that can profoundly impact their professional and personal lives.

4.7 Chapter Summary

Fraud has far-reaching implications for various stakeholders within nonprofit organizations, encompassing financial assets, vendors, government entities, and employees. Firstly, fraudulent activities within nonprofits can lead to significant losses of financial assets. It may compromise the organization's ability to achieve its mission and serve its beneficiaries effectively. Misappropriation of funds, embezzlement, and falsification of financial records deplete resources and erode trust among donors and funding partners. This loss of trust can result in decreased contributions and support, further exacerbating the organization's financial challenges and hindering its ability to sustain vital programs and initiatives.

Secondly, fraud can harm the organization's relationships with its vendors and suppliers. fraud can tarnish vendors' reputations and credibility if they become associated with fraudulent activities perpetrated by the nonprofit. This can lead to strained business relationships, increased scrutiny of transactions, and potential legal and regulatory implications for the vendors. Ultimately, the implications of fraud on vendors extend beyond financial losses to include reputational damage and operational disruptions.

Lastly, fraud within nonprofit organizations can have profound implications for government entities tasked with oversight and regulation. Misuse of government funds, misreporting of program outcomes, and regulatory non-compliance can undermine public trust in government institutions and raise questions about the effectiveness of existing regulatory frameworks. This may result in increased regulatory scrutiny, audits, and enforcement actions. It may also impose additional administrative burdens and compliance costs on the nonprofit organization and the government. Furthermore, fraud within nonprofits may prompt government entities to reassess their funding allocations and oversight mechanisms to prevent future occurrences. It may also impact the organization's access to government grants and contracts.

Overall, the implications of fraud on financial assets, vendors, government, and employees underscore the critical need for robust internal controls, ethical leadership, and transparency within nonprofit organizations to safeguard their integrity and sustainability.

4.8 Case Study: Implications of Fraud on HealthSouth Corporation (NGO)

Background: HealthSouth Corporation was a large healthcare provider specializing in rehabilitation services, operating numerous hospitals, clinics, and outpatient centers across the United States. Dedicated to providing healthcare services to underserved communities, it recently faced a scandal involving widespread fraudulent activities that had significant implications for its financial assets and all stakeholders involved. The organization relied heavily on government grants, donations from individual and corporate donors, and partnerships with vendors to sustain its operations and deliver essential healthcare services to vulnerable populations.

Fraudulent Activities: The scandal erupted in 2003 when the Securities and Exchange Commission (SEC) filed fraud charges against HealthSouth and its CEO, Richard Scrushy. The allegations centered on a massive accounting fraud scheme orchestrated by top executives, including Scrushy, to artificially inflate the company's earnings and stock price.

Key elements of fraud included:

1. **Inflated Revenue**: HealthSouth executives engaged in fraudulent accounting practices, such as recording fake revenue and inflating

the company's financial statements to meet earnings targets and impress investors.

2. **False Assets:** The company falsified its assets and accounts receivable, overstating the value of its assets to deceive investors and creditors about the company's financial health.

3. **Manipulated Expenses**: HealthSouth executives manipulated expenses, such as understating costs and overestimating assets, to maintain the appearance of profitability and financial stability.

4. **Corporate Governance Failures**: There were significant failures in corporate governance, with executives bypassing internal controls and oversight mechanisms to perpetrate fraud.

These fraudulent activities depleted the organization's financial resources and undermined its ability to deliver critical healthcare services to those in need.

Implications for HealthSouth and its stakeholders:

1. Financial Losses: The fraudulent activities led to significant financial losses for investors, employees, and creditors as the company's true financial condition became apparent. Stock

prices plummeted, and the company faced bankruptcy proceedings.

2. Legal Repercussions: Several HealthSouth executives, including CEO Richard Scrushy, faced criminal charges and were convicted of fraud-related offenses. Scrushy was ultimately sentenced to prison, and the company paid substantial fines to settle civil lawsuits and regulatory enforcement actions.

3. Reputational Damage: The scandal tarnished HealthSouth's reputation as a trusted healthcare provider dedicated to serving underserved communities. The company's brand suffered irreparable damage, leading to a loss of trust among patients, employees, and the broader public.

4. Impact on Healthcare Services: The fallout from the scandal disrupted healthcare services provided by HealthSouth facilities, raising concerns about the continuity of care for patients, especially those in underserved communities who relied on the organization for essential rehabilitation services [1].

----
[1] U.S. Securities and Exchange Commission (SEC). (2003). HealthSouth Corporation and Richard M. Scrushy. Retrieved from https://www.sec.gov/litigation/litreleases/lr-18044.

Response and Recovery: In response to the scandal, HealthSouth underwent significant restructuring and implemented reforms to enhance transparency, accountability, and corporate governance. However, the HealthSouth scandal is a cautionary tale about the dangers of corporate fraud and the importance of ethical leadership and oversight in nonprofit organizations dedicated to providing essential healthcare services to vulnerable populations.

Section 2: Responsibility

Introduction

Fraud poses a significant threat to the integrity and effectiveness of nonprofit organizations. Then, the responsibility of detecting and preventing it is paramount for everyone to help the organization fulfill its missions and serve communities. In the complex landscape of the nonprofit sector, where resources are often scarce and stakeholders' trust is paramount, detecting and preventing fraud requires a collective effort from all involved parties. Managers, employees, donors, vendors, and government entities each play a critical role in safeguarding against fraudulent activities and upholding the principles of transparency, accountability, and ethical conduct.

Responsibility of Managers

Organizational managers at the forefront of fraud prevention efforts are primarily responsible for establishing a culture of integrity and implementing robust internal controls. Managers must cultivate an environment where ethical behavior is encouraged, actively promoted, and rewarded. This involves providing clear guidance on acceptable conduct, fostering open communication channels for reporting suspicious activities, and leading by example through their adherence to ethical standards. For example, managers should use:

Strategic Planning: Developing and implementing a comprehensive anti-fraud strategy that aligns with the organization's goals. This includes establishing clear policies, risk assessments, and procedures for reporting and handling fraud.

Regular Meetings: Schedule and lead meetings to review anti-fraud measures, discuss vulnerabilities, and assess compliance with established protocols. Managers should foster an open environment for discussing concerns.

Training: Ensure employees receive regular training on fraud awareness, detection, and reporting procedures. Managers should facilitate access to resources and expert-led sessions. Furthermore, managers must ensure that adequate oversight mechanisms are in place to monitor financial transactions, procurement processes, and program activities, thereby mitigating the risk of fraud occurring undetected.

Responsibility of Employees

Employees are the frontline defense against fraud within nonprofit organizations, as they are often the first to observe irregularities or discrepancies in day-to-day operations. Employees need to be vigilant and proactive in identifying potential red flags or warning signs of fraudulent activities. This requires ongoing training and education to increase awareness of common fraud schemes, as well as clear protocols for reporting suspicions or concerns to management or designated compliance officers. For example, employees should use:

Adherence to Policies: Follow the organization's anti-fraud policies and procedures diligently. Employees should be aware of the signs of fraud and how to report suspicious activities.

Participation in Meetings: Engage in regular meetings by providing feedback and sharing observations about potential risks or areas for improvement.

Continuous Learning: Attend training sessions to stay informed about the latest fraud schemes and prevention techniques. Employees should cultivate a culture of integrity and accountability. Additionally, fostering a culture where employees feel empowered to speak up without fear of retaliation is crucial for early detection and intervention in cases of fraud.

Responsibility of Donors, Vendors, and Government

Beyond the internal stakeholders of nonprofit organizations, external parties such as donors, vendors, and government entities also bear responsibility for detecting and preventing fraud. Donors play a critical role in holding nonprofits accountable for the responsible stewardship of their contributions by conducting due diligence, asking probing questions about financial management practices, and demanding transparency in reporting. For example, donors should:

Due Diligence: Donors should conduct thorough research on the organizations they support, including reviewing financial statements, audit reports, and anti-fraud measures in place. They should also ask questions about how funds are managed and allocated.

Encourage Transparency: Demand transparency from the organizations they support regarding fund usage and reporting. Donors can advocate for regular updates and disclosures.

Support for Training Initiatives: Consider funding or supporting training programs that enhance anti-fraud controls within the organization, thereby fostering a culture of accountability.

Similarly, vendors should exercise caution when engaging with nonprofits, ensuring that contracts and transactions follow ethical standards and legal requirements. Government entities, as regulators and funding partners, have a vested interest in ensuring the integrity of nonprofits receiving public funds.

They should, therefore, robust oversight mechanisms and hold organizations accountable for compliance with regulatory standards. For example, government leaders should use:

Regulatory Oversight: Establish and enforce regulations that require nonprofits to implement anti-fraud measures and maintain financial transparency. This includes conducting audits and inspections to ensure compliance.

Collaboration: Work with nonprofit organizations to share best practices and provide resources for developing effective anti-fraud strategies. Government officials can facilitate training programs and workshops.

Funding Accountability: Monitor how public funds and donations are used within nonprofit organizations, ensuring that there is accountability for financial practices and outcomes.

Fig3. Collaboration and Engagement   Source: Google Images

Preventing and detecting fraud in nonprofit organizations requires a collaborative effort involving managers, employees, donors, vendors, and government entities.

By fostering a culture of integrity, promoting transparency and accountability, and implementing effective oversight mechanisms, nonprofits can mitigate the risk of fraud and uphold the trust of their stakeholders in their mission and operations.

Moreover, collaboration among managers, employees, donors, and government officials is crucial for effectively combating fraud in nonprofit organizations. All stakeholders need to work together to establish clear responsibilities. For instance, they can develop strategic planning, regular meetings, and training to create a practical framework for fraud prevention. They should also ensure the effective use of all organization resources to achieve its mission successfully.

Chapter 5
Fraud Detection

5.1 Introduction

Detecting fraud in nonprofit organizations is critical, given their reliance on public trust and charitable donations to fulfill their missions. Nonprofits often operate with limited resources and rely heavily on volunteers and donors, making them particularly vulnerable to fraudulent activities. Instances of fraud in these organizations can have severe repercussions, tarnishing their reputations and impeding their ability to serve their intended beneficiaries effectively. Thus, implementing robust fraud detection measures is essential to safeguarding the integrity and sustainability of nonprofit operations.

Nonprofit organizations face unique challenges when it comes to fraud detection. These challenges include complex financial structures, diverse revenue streams, and decentralized decision-making processes.[1] Unlike for-profit entities, where financial gains are a primary motive for fraud, motives for fraudulent activities in nonprofits vary widely, ranging from personal enrichment to circumventing regulatory requirements. Consequently, detecting fraud in these organizations requires a multifaceted approach that considers financial discrepancies and behavioral indicators.[2] By proactively addressing these challenges and implementing comprehensive fraud detection strategies, nonprofits can uphold their commitment to transparency and accountability. Then, they can preserve public trust and ensure the effective fulfillment of their missions.

5.2 How to Detect Fraud?

Detecting fraud in nonprofit organizations requires a combination of proactive measures, diligent oversight, and effective monitoring systems. Here are several key strategies to detect fraud in nonprofit organizations:

1. **Implement Strong Internal Controls**: Establish robust internal controls that segregate duties, ensure proper transaction authorization, and institute checks and

---

[1] Luamba, D., Chagadama, J., Blye, M. L., James, K. C., & Jaman, S. H. (2022). Strategies for Ensuring Small Businesses Longevity: A Qualitative Study.
[2] Joel Chagadama, D. B. A., & Luamba, D. S. (2023). Cyberattacks: A Huge Concern for Small Business Sustainability.

balances within the organization's financial processes. This can help prevent fraudulent activities and facilitate the detection of irregularities.

2. **Conduct Regular Financial Reviews and Audits**: Regular financial reviews and audits conducted by independent parties can help uncover discrepancies, errors, or suspicious transactions. These reviews should encompass various aspects of the organization's financial operations, including expenditures, revenue sources, payroll, and compliance with regulatory requirements.

3. **Monitor Financial Statements and Budgets**: Regularly review financial statements, budgets, and cash flow projections to identify any inconsistencies or deviations from expected norms. Analyze variances and trends to detect unusual patterns indicating fraudulent activities, such as unauthorized expenses or revenue misappropriation [1].

4. **Train Staff and Volunteers:** Train staff, volunteers, and board members to recognize red flags and report suspicious activities. Encourage a culture of transparency and accountability where individuals feel empowered to raise concerns without fear of retaliation.

---

[1] Joel Chagadama, D. B. A., & Luamba, D. S. (2023). Cyberattacks: A Huge Concern for Small Business Sustainability

5. **Conduct Due Diligence on Vendors and Partners**: Perform due diligence on vendors, contractors, and other partners to verify their legitimacy and ensure compliance with contractual agreements. Scrutinize invoices and contracts for discrepancies or signs of fraudulent billing practices.

6. **Monitor Donor Contributions**: Implement procedures to monitor and reconcile donor contributions, including online donations, grants, and fundraising events. Verify the legitimacy of donors and track the flow of funds to identify any irregularities or potential misappropriation of donations.

7. **Utilize Technology and Data Analytics:** Leverage technology and data analytics tools to automate fraud detection processes and efficiently analyze large volumes of financial data. Monitor transactional data for anomalies, conduct trend analysis, and utilize predictive modeling to identify potential fraud risks [1].

8. **Establish Whistleblower Policies**: Establish clear whistleblower policies and confidential reporting mechanisms to encourage individuals to report suspected fraud or misconduct without fear of reprisal. Ensure that reports are thoroughly investigated and addressed

---

[1] Luamba, D. (2019). Strategies small business owners use to remain sustainable (Doctoral dissertation, Walden University).

promptly to prevent further harm to the organization.

By implementing these proactive measures and maintaining a vigilant stance against fraud, nonprofit organizations can detect and prevent fraudulent activities. They can also safeguard their assets and uphold their commitments to donors, beneficiaries, and stakeholders.[1]

5.3 Who Detects Fraud?

In nonprofit organizations, the responsibility for detecting fraud typically falls on multiple organizational stakeholders. Here are the key parties involved in fraud detection:

1. **Board of Directors:** The board of directors oversees the organization's operations, including financial management and compliance. Boards are responsible for establishing policies and procedures to prevent and detect fraud, hiring competent leadership, and regularly reviewing financial reports and audit findings. They should actively inquire about the organization's financial health and ask probing questions to uncover any signs of irregularities or misconduct.

---

[1] Raval, V. (2020). Corporate governance: A pragmatic guide for auditors, directors, investors, and accountants. CRC Press.

2. **Executive Leadership:** Executive leadership, including the executive director or CEO, holds responsibility for implementing internal controls, fostering a culture of transparency and accountability, and ensuring compliance with legal and regulatory requirements. They oversee day-to-day operations, monitor financial activities, and promptly address any concerns or red flags related to fraud.

3. **Finance and Accounting Department:** The finance and accounting department is directly involved in managing the organization's finances, recording transactions, and preparing financial statements. Staff members in this department enforce internal controls, reconcile accounts, and conduct regular financial reviews to detect discrepancies or anomalies that may indicate fraudulent activities.

4. **Internal Audit Team:** Some nonprofit organizations have internal audit functions tasked with independently evaluating the effectiveness of internal controls. These functions assess compliance with policies and procedures and identify areas of risk or vulnerability to fraud. Internal auditors also conduct periodic audits and investigations to detect fraud and provide recommendations for strengthening controls and mitigating risks.

5. **External Auditors:** Nonprofit organizations engage external auditors, typically independent accounting firms, to conduct annual audits or financial reviews. They perform an independent assessment of the organization's financial statements, internal controls, and compliance with accounting standards and regulatory requirements. External auditors are responsible for detecting material misstatements, errors, or instances of fraud and providing assurance to stakeholders about the accuracy and integrity of the financial information presented.

6. **Staff and Volunteers:** All staff members and volunteers within the organization play a role in fraud detection by adhering to policies and procedures. They also report any suspicions or concerns about fraudulent activities and maintain ethical conduct in their interactions with donors, vendors, and beneficiaries.

By engaging multiple stakeholders and fostering a culture of vigilance and accountability, nonprofit organizations can enhance their capacity to detect and prevent fraud effectively. Collaboration among board members, executive leadership, internal and external auditors, and staff members is essential to safeguarding the organization's assets and preserving its reputation and trustworthiness.

5.4 Why Detect Fraud?

Detecting fraud in nonprofit organizations is essential for several reasons:

Preserving Trust and Reputation: Nonprofit organizations rely heavily on public trust and confidence to fulfill their missions effectively. Fraud can damage their reputation and erode the trust of donors, volunteers, beneficiaries, and other stakeholders. Detecting and addressing fraud promptly helps maintain transparency, integrity, and credibility. It also helps safeguard the organization's reputation and ensure continued support from the community.

Protecting Assets and Resources: Nonprofits often operate with limited resources and rely on donations, grants, and other funding sources to sustain their operations and programs. Fraudulent activities such as embezzlement, misappropriation of funds, or fraudulent billing can deplete valuable resources meant for charitable purposes. Detecting fraud helps protect the organization's assets and ensures that resources are used efficiently and ethically to advance its mission and serve its beneficiaries.

Compliance with Legal and Regulatory Requirements: Nonprofit organizations are subject to various legal and regulatory requirements governing their operations, financial reporting, and governance practices. Failure to detect and prevent fraud can lead to legal and regulatory consequences, including fines, penalties, loss of tax-exempt status, and reputational damage. Detecting fraud helps ensure compliance with laws and regulations. It also helps mitigate the risk of legal liabilities and sanctions.

Strengthening Internal Controls and Governance: Detecting fraud prompts organizations to review and strengthen their internal controls, policies, and governance structures. By identifying weaknesses or vulnerabilities that allow fraudulent activities, nonprofits can implement corrective measures to prevent future occurrences and enhance their overall governance and risk management practices.

Maintaining Donor and Stakeholder Confidence: Donors, volunteers, and other stakeholders expect nonprofit organizations to uphold high standards of transparency, accountability, and ethical conduct. Detecting and addressing fraud demonstrates the organization's commitment to responsible stewardship of resources and reinforces confidence among donors and stakeholders. Maintaining trust and credibility is crucial for sustaining support and engagement from the community over the long term.

Detecting fraud in nonprofit organizations is imperative for preserving trust, protecting assets, ensuring compliance, strengthening governance, and maintaining donor confidence [1].

By actively addressing fraud risks and fostering a culture of integrity and accountability, nonprofits can uphold their mission-driven objectives and maximize their positive impact on society.

5.5   Where to Detect Fraud?

Detecting fraud in nonprofit organizations involves monitoring various aspects of the organization's operations and financial activities. Several key areas where nonprofit organizations' efforts should focus include:

Financial Transactions: Monitoring financial transactions is critical for detecting fraudulent activities such as embezzlement, unauthorized expenditures, or fraudulent billing. This includes scrutinizing invoices, expense reports, bank statements, and other financial records for inconsistencies, irregularities, or unauthorized transactions.

Donations and Fundraising: Nonprofit organizations rely on donations and fundraising activities to support their programs and initiatives.

---

[1] Blye, M. L., & Luamba, D. (2021). Fraud in nonprofit organizations: How to mitigate it. *International Journal of Business and Management*, 4, 385-392.

Detecting fraud in this area involves verifying the legitimacy of donors, tracking the flow of funds, and ensuring that donations align with their intended purposes. This also includes monitoring fundraising events, online donations, and grant funding for any signs of misappropriation or diversion of funds.

Employee and Volunteer Activities: Fraudulent activities can also occur internally, involving employees or volunteers who may exploit their positions for personal gain. Monitoring employee and volunteer activities, such as payroll processing, timekeeping, and reimbursement claims, can help detect instances of fraud such as payroll fraud, ghost employees, or false reimbursement requests.

Procurement and Contracts: Nonprofits often enter into contracts with vendors, consultants, and service providers to fulfill their operational needs. Detecting fraud in procurement involves scrutinizing contracts, purchase orders, and vendor invoices for signs of inflated costs, kickbacks, or conflicts of interest. Monitoring the procurement process and conducting due diligence on vendors can help mitigate the risk of fraudulent activities.

Grant Management: Nonprofit organizations that receive grants from government agencies, foundations, or other sources must ensure compliance with grant requirements and guidelines.

Detecting fraud in grant management involves monitoring grant expenditures, reporting processes, and program outcomes to identify any discrepancies or misrepresentations. This includes verifying the accuracy of grant proposals, budget allocations, and programmatic achievements.

Internal Controls and Governance: Strong internal controls and governance structures are essential for preventing and detecting fraud in nonprofit organizations. This includes establishing policies and procedures, segregating duties, conducting regular audits and reviews, and providing fraud awareness and prevention training. Monitoring the effectiveness of internal controls and governance mechanisms can help identify areas of weakness or vulnerability to fraudulent activities.

By focusing on these key areas and implementing proactive fraud detection measures, nonprofit organizations can mitigate the risk of fraud. They can also protect their assets and resources and uphold their commitments to transparency, accountability, and ethical conduct.

5.6   When to Detect Fraud

Detecting fraud in nonprofit organizations is an ongoing process that requires continuous monitoring and vigilance.[1] While it's crucial to be proactive in

---

[1] Solomon, A. N., Emmanuel, O. O., Ajibade, D. S., & Emmanuel, D. M. (2023). Assessing the effectiveness of internal control systems on fraud prevention and detection of selected public institutions of Ekiti State, Nigeria. *Asian Journal of Economics, Finance and Management*, 231-244.

identifying fraudulent activities, there are specific times and occasions to detect fraud:

Regularly Scheduled Audits and Reviews: Nonprofit organizations should conduct regular financial audits and reviews, typically annually or semi-annually, to assess the accuracy of financial records, internal controls, and compliance with policies and regulations. These audits allow one to detect irregularities or suspicious activities that may indicate fraud.

During Periods of Organizational Change: Organizational change, such as leadership transitions, restructuring, or program expansion, can create vulnerabilities that may be exploited by individuals engaging in fraudulent activities. Therefore, it's essential to intensify fraud detection efforts during these periods to mitigate risks and ensure proper controls are in place.

After Significant Events or Transactions: Following significant events or transactions, such as large fundraising campaigns, mergers or acquisitions, or major changes in funding sources, organizations should conduct thorough reviews to ensure the integrity of financial reporting and the proper use of funds. These events may present opportunities for fraud or misappropriation, making heightened vigilance necessary.

Upon Detection of Red Flags or Warning Signs: Red flags or warning signs may indicate potential fraud, such as unexplained discrepancies in financial records, unusually high expenses, or reports of suspicious behavior from employees or stakeholders. When such indicators occur, immediate action should be taken to investigate and address the underlying issues.[1]

Regular Training and Awareness Programs: Ongoing training and awareness programs on fraud prevention and detection for staff, volunteers, and board members are crucial for fraud detection. These programs help educate individuals about the types of fraud that may occur, how to recognize warning signs and the importance of reporting suspicions promptly.

During External Reviews or Assessments: External reviews of agencies, funding organizations, or independent auditors provide additional opportunities to detect fraud.[1] Nonprofit organizations should cooperate fully with external reviewers or controllers and ensure all necessary documentation and information are readily available for examination.

In essence, there is no specific moment to detect fraud, but rather, fraud detection requires a continuous and proactive approach. By integrating fraud detection efforts into regular operations,

---

[1] Solomon, A. N., Emmanuel, O. O., Ajibade, D. S., & Emmanuel, D. M. (2023). Assessing the effectiveness of internal control systems on fraud prevention and detection of selected public institutions of Ekiti State, Nigeria. *Asian Journal of Economics, Finance and Management*, 231-244.

organizations can minimize risks, protect their assets, and uphold their commitments to transparency and accountability. [1]

5.7 Chapter Summary

Fraud detection is a critical process aimed at identifying and addressing fraudulent activities within organizations. Fraud detection encompasses various strategies and methods focused on understanding how fraud occurs, why it happens, where it occurs, when it takes place, and who may be involved.

How: Fraud detection involves implementing robust internal controls, regularly monitoring financial transactions, and using technology and data analytics to identify anomalies or suspicious patterns. Nonprofit organizations can uncover fraudulent activities and mitigate risks by analyzing financial records, conducting audits, and scrutinizing internal processes.

Why: Detecting fraud is essential for preserving trust, protecting assets, and ensuring compliance with legal and regulatory requirements. Fraudulent activities can have severe consequences, including reputational damage, financial losses, and legal liabilities. By detecting and addressing fraud promptly, organizations can minimize these risks and maintain their credibility and integrity.

---

[1] Kimmel, P.D., Weygandt, J.J., & Kieso, D.E. (2013). *Financial accounting: Tools for Business Decision making* (7th ed.). Danvers, MA: John Wiley & Sons, Inc.

Where: Fraud can occur in various organizational areas, including financial transactions, donations and fundraising, employee activities, procurement and contracts, grant management, and internal controls and governance structures. Monitoring these key areas is essential for effectively detecting and preventing fraudulent activities.

When: Fraud can occur anytime, making ongoing monitoring and proactive detection measures crucial. Organizations should conduct regular reviews, audits, and risk assessments to identify potential fraud risks and respond promptly to any red flags or warning signs.

Who: Fraud detection efforts involve multiple organizational stakeholders, including the board of directors, executive leadership, finance and accounting personnel, internal auditors, external auditors, staff, and volunteers. Collaboration among these parties is essential for fostering a culture of integrity and accountability and ensuring effective fraud detection and prevention.

In summary, fraud detection is a multifaceted process that requires vigilance, diligence, and collaboration across the organization. By understanding how, why, where, when, and who may be involved in fraudulent activities, nonprofit organizations can implement proactive measures to mitigate risks, protect their assets, and uphold their commitments to transparency and ethical conduct by understanding how, why, where, when, and who may be involved in fraudulent activities.

5.8 Case Study: Detecting Fraud in Family Resource Center

Background

Family Resource Center is a nonprofit organization that provides resources and support to low-income families and individuals in SAN DIEGO neighborhood communities. With a mission to promote social lives for needy people, the foundation relies heavily on donations from individuals, corporations, and grants from government agencies. As the foundation's operations expanded, concerns arose about the potential risk of fraud within the organization.

Who

The finance department, internal auditors, and Internal Revenue Services (IRS) investigators detected fraud at the Family Resource Center Foundation. The team collaborated closely with the board of directors and owners to conduct thorough investigations and implement proactive measures to detect it.

When

Fraud detection efforts were intensified during the annual financial audit and at various points throughout the year, including after significant fundraising events or organizational changes.

Additionally, regular reviews of financial transactions and internal controls were conducted to identify any anomalies or irregularities that may indicate fraudulent activities.

Where

Fraud detection efforts were focused on multiple areas within the organization, including financial transactions, donor contributions, grant management, procurement processes, and employee activities. Specifically, attention was given to scrutinizing expense reports, vendor invoices, payroll records, and donor contributions for any signs of fraudulent behavior.

How

Fraud detection was facilitated through a combination of strategies, including data analysis, forensic accounting techniques, whistleblower hotlines, and internal control assessments. Data analytics tools were used to identify patterns or anomalies in financial transactions, while forensic accountants conducted in-depth examinations of financial records to trace potentially fraudulent activities. Internal controls were also strengthened, and staff members were trained to recognize red flags and promptly report suspicions.

Why

Detecting fraud was essential for protecting the foundation's assets, preserving donor trust, and upholding its reputation and credibility. By identifying and addressing fraudulent activities, the organization could minimize financial losses, mitigate legal and regulatory risks, and ensure that resources were used efficiently to advance its mission of supporting underprivileged children.

Outcome

Through diligent efforts and proactive measures, several instances of fraud were identified and addressed within The Family Resource Center. The owners (husband and wife) were found guilty and sentenced to 9 months and 15 months in prison for fund misuse. These included using the tax-exempt charity as their personal bank account and evading their tax obligations, then cheating the IRS by failing to pay over $50,000 in taxes over a million dollars gained from fraud.[1] By promptly detecting fraudulent activities, the IRS found the organization guilty. It was instructed to strengthen its internal controls, enhance transparency, and reinforce its commitment to ethical conduct and accountability.

---

[1] Department of Justice (DOJ). (2020). Charity Founders Sentenced to Prison for Using Non-Profit to Steal from Donors and Cheat on Their Taxes. Retrieved https:https://www.justice.gov/usao-sdca/pr/charity-founders-sentenced-prison-using-non-profit

Conclusion

Detecting fraud in nonprofit organizations requires a concerted effort involving various stakeholders and proactive measures. By focusing on the who, when, where, how, and why of fraud detection, nonprofit organizations can safeguard their assets, protect donor trust, and fulfill their mission effectively. Through continuous vigilance and collaboration, nonprofits can minimize the risk of fraud and uphold their commitments to transparency, integrity, and accountability.

Chapter 6

Prevention of Fraud in Nonprofit Organizations

6.1 Introduction

Fraud prevention is an essential pillar in nonprofit organizations' operations, pivoting in safeguarding their integrity, preserving donor trust, and ensuring the effective allocation of resources toward their charitable endeavors. The imperative to prevent fraud in nonprofits organizations stems from their reliance on public goodwill and the ethical stewardship of funds generously donated for noble causes. By proactively addressing fraud risks, nonprofits can uphold their commitments to transparency and accountability, bolstering their credibility and sustaining their mission-driven impact.

Preventing fraud in nonprofit organizations necessitates a multifaceted approach encompassing various strategies to mitigate the unique risks and vulnerabilities inherent in their operations. This involves establishing robust internal controls, conducting regular audits and reviews, fostering a culture of ethical conduct and accountability, and leveraging technology to enhance detection capabilities. Moreover, emphasizing fraud prevention efforts during organizational change, such as leadership transitions or expansion initiatives, and focusing on critical financial transactions, donor contributions, grant management, and employee activities are crucial to fortifying the organization's resilience against fraudulent activities. Through a comprehensive and vigilant approach to fraud prevention, nonprofit organizations can uphold their commitments to their beneficiaries, donors, and the broader community, ensuring their charitable missions' effective and ethical pursuit.[1]

6.2 How To Prevent Fraud?

Preventing fraud in nonprofit organizations requires a proactive and comprehensive approach to address the unique risks and vulnerabilities inherent in their operations. Here are several strategies to prevent fraud in nonprofit organizations:

---
[1] Stamler, R., Marschdorf, H., & Possamai, M. (2014). *Fraud Prevention and Detection*. Routledge.

Establish Robust Internal Controls: Implement strong internal controls to safeguard assets and prevent opportunities for fraud. This includes segregating duties, requiring dual authorization for financial transactions, conducting regular reconciliations, and maintaining strict oversight over financial processes.

Conduct Regular Audits and Reviews: Schedule regular financial audits and reviews conducted by independent parties to assess the effectiveness of internal controls, detect any irregularities or anomalies, and ensure compliance with regulatory requirements. Internal audits should be performed periodically to evaluate specific risk areas and identify improvement opportunities.[1]

Foster a Culture of Ethical Conduct: Cultivate a culture of integrity, transparency, and accountability throughout the organization. Provide ethics training and awareness programs to staff, volunteers, and board members to promote ethical decision-making and encourage individuals to report any suspicions of fraud promptly.

Leverage Technology and Data Analytics: Use technology and data analytics tools to enhance fraud detection capabilities. Implement fraud detection software to monitor financial transactions for

---

[1] Turner, P. (2022). *Complementarity in Organizations: Strategy, Leadership, Management, Talent and Engagement in the Fourth Industrial Revolution.* Springer Nature.

anomalies or suspicious patterns. Conduct data analysis to identify trends and outliers that may indicate fraudulent activities.

Implement Whistleblower Policies: Establish clear whistleblower policies and confidential reporting mechanisms to encourage individuals to report suspected fraud or misconduct without fear of retaliation. Ensure that reports are thoroughly investigated and addressed promptly to prevent further harm to the organization.[1]

Conduct Due Diligence on Vendors and Partners: Perform due diligence on vendors, contractors, and other partners to verify their legitimacy and ensure compliance with contractual agreements. Scrutinize contracts and invoices for discrepancies or signs of fraudulent billing practices.

Monitor Donor Contributions: Implement procedures to monitor and reconcile donor contributions, including online donations, grants, and fundraising events. Verify the legitimacy of donors and track the flow of funds to identify any irregularities or potential misappropriation of donations.

Stay Informed about Fraud Risks: Stay informed about emerging fraud risks and trends within the

----
[1] Peltier-Rivest, D. (2018). The battle against fraud: do reporting mechanisms work? *Journal of Financial Crime, 25*(3), 784-794.

nonprofit sector. Participate in industry conferences, workshops, and training sessions to learn about best practices in fraud prevention and share knowledge with peers and colleagues.

By implementing these proactive measures and maintaining a vigilant stance against fraud, nonprofit organizations can minimize the risk of fraudulent activities, protect their assets and resources, and uphold their commitments to transparency, integrity, and accountability.

6.3 Who Should Prevent Fraud?

Preventing fraud is crucial to maintaining trust among donors, supporters, and the community at large in nonprofit organizations. While everyone involved in the organization ultimately has responsibility for preventing fraud, some key individuals and entities play particularly significant roles in fraud prevention.[1] First and foremost, the board of directors of a nonprofit organization holds a fiduciary duty to oversee the organization's finances and operations. This includes implementing strong internal controls and financial oversight mechanisms to deter and detect fraudulent activities.

Boards should regularly review financial statements, budgets, and internal audit reports to ensure transparency and accountability. Additionally, they

---
[1] Mandal, A., & S, A. (2023). Preventing financial statement fraud in the corporate sector: insights from auditors. *Journal of Financial Reporting and Accounting.*

should establish a culture of ethical conduct and set clear expectations for integrity throughout the organization.

Nonprofit executives and management also bear responsibility for preventing fraud within their organizations. They are tasked with implementing and enforcing policies and procedures designed to mitigate the risk of fraud. This includes segregating duties, conducting thorough background checks on employees and volunteers, and providing regular training on fraud awareness and prevention. Executives should lead by example, demonstrating a commitment to ethical behavior and accountability in all aspects of the organization's operations.

Furthermore, external stakeholders such as donors, regulators, and auditors play vital roles in preventing fraud in nonprofit organizations. Donors should conduct due diligence before making contributions, ensuring that the organizations they support have sound financial management practices in place. Regulators, such as state attorneys general and the Internal Revenue Service (IRS), enforce compliance with laws and regulations governing nonprofit organizations, imposing penalties on those found to engage in fraudulent activities. Auditors provide independent assessments of an organization's financial statements and internal controls, helping to identify potential areas of risk and offering recommendations for improvement.

In essence, preventing fraud in nonprofit organizations requires a collaborative effort involving the board of directors, executives, employees, donors, regulators, and auditors. By fostering a culture of transparency, accountability, and ethical behavior, nonprofit organizations can effectively deter and detect fraudulent activities, safeguarding their missions and the trust of their stakeholders.

6.4 Why Preventing Fraud?

Preventing fraud in nonprofit organizations is essential for several reasons, all of which underscore the significance of maintaining trust, integrity, and accountability within these entities.

Firstly, nonprofit organizations operate on a foundation of public trust and reliance. Donors contribute resources, whether financial or in-kind, with the expectation that these resources will be used to fulfill the organization's mission and serve the intended beneficiaries. Fraud undermines this trust by diverting resources from their intended purposes, potentially harming those relying on the organization's services. The loss of trust resulting from fraud can have far-reaching consequences, including reduced donations, diminished support, and reputational damage that may impact the organization's ability to achieve its goals.[1]

Secondly, nonprofit organizations often rely heavily on public funding, grants, and donations to sustain their operations. Fraudulent activities, such as embezzlement, misappropriation of funds, or falsifying financial records, not only squander valuable resources but also jeopardize the organization's eligibility for future funding. Government agencies, foundations, and other grant-making entities typically require strict adherence to financial accountability standards and may revoke funding or impose sanctions if fraud is detected. Preventing fraud is, therefore, crucial for safeguarding the financial viability and sustainability of nonprofit organizations, ensuring they can continue to fulfill their missions effectively.

Lastly, nonprofit organizations play vital roles in addressing social, environmental, and humanitarian challenges, often serving vulnerable populations, or advocating for marginalized communities. Fraud detracts from these efforts by diverting resources away from programs and services that directly benefit those in need. Every dollar lost to fraud represents a missed opportunity to make a positive impact and advance the organization's mission. By preventing fraud, nonprofit organizations can maximize the

---

[1] Branet, D. S., & Hategan, C. D. (2024). Bibliometric Framing of Research Trends Regarding Public Sector Auditing to Fight Corruption and Prevent Fraud. *Journal of Risk and Financial Management*, 17(3), 94.

impact of their resources, ensuring that they reach the individuals and communities they are intended to serve.

In conclusion, preventing fraud in nonprofit organizations is imperative for upholding trust, maintaining financial integrity, and maximizing social impact. By implementing robust internal controls, fostering a culture of transparency and accountability, and prioritizing ethical conduct, nonprofit organizations can safeguard their resources, preserve their reputations, and fulfill their commitments to their stakeholders and communities.

6.5 Where to Prevent Fraud?

Fraud prevention in nonprofit organizations should not only focus on specific locations but encompass all areas where fraudulent activities can occur. However, it's essential to recognize that certain locations within an organization may present higher risks for fraud due to factors such as the handling of sensitive information, the flow of funds, or the level of oversight. Here are some key locations or departments within nonprofit organizations where fraud prevention measures should be particularly emphasized:

Finance Department: The finance department is often a focal point for fraud prevention efforts due to its role in managing financial transactions, budgeting, and accounting. If proper controls and oversight are not in place, embezzlement, falsification of financial records, or unauthorized expenditures can occur within this department. Preventive measures such as segregation of duties, regular audits, and reconciliations should be implemented to deter and detect fraudulent activities.

Fundraising and Development Offices: Fundraising and development offices are responsible for soliciting donations, managing donor relationships, and organizing fundraising events. Fraudulent activities in these areas may include misrepresenting fundraising efforts, diversion of funds, or misusing donor information. Nonprofit organizations should implement safeguards to ensure the integrity of fundraising activities, including transparent reporting on fundraising outcomes and protecting donor data from unauthorized access or exploitation.

Program Delivery Sites: Nonprofit organizations deliver programs and services through various sites or locations, such as community centers, shelters, or outreach facilities. These locations may be susceptible to fraud related to the misappropriation of resources, diversion of donations or supplies, or fraudulent reporting of program outcomes. Strong oversight, monitoring, and evaluation mechanisms should be in place to prevent and detect fraudulent activities at program delivery sites.

Administrative Offices: Administrative offices encompass functions such as human resources, procurement, and general administration, where fraudulent activities such as payroll fraud, vendor fraud, or conflicts of interest may occur. Nonprofit organizations should establish clear policies and procedures governing administrative operations, conduct background checks on employees and vendors, and implement controls to mitigate the risk of fraud in these areas.

While these locations highlight potential risk areas for fraud in nonprofit organizations, it's crucial to adopt a comprehensive approach to fraud prevention that addresses vulnerabilities across the entire organization. By promoting a culture of integrity, implementing robust internal controls, and fostering transparency and accountability at all levels, nonprofits can reduce the likelihood of fraudulent activities and safeguard their mission and reputation.

6.6 Chapter Summary

Preventing fraud in nonprofit organizations involves various stakeholders, strategies, and measures to safeguard the organization's resources, reputation, and mission.

Who

Preventing fraud in nonprofit organizations requires the involvement and commitment of all stakeholders, including board members, executives, staff, donors, regulators, and auditors. Each stakeholder plays a critical role in implementing fraud prevention measures and fostering a culture of integrity and accountability within the organization.

Why

Fraud prevention is essential for nonprofit organizations to maintain public trust, uphold financial integrity, and maximize their social impact. Fraud undermines trust among donors, volunteers, and the community, jeopardizes funding opportunities, and detracts from the organization's ability to fulfill its mission effectively.

When

Fraud prevention efforts should be ongoing and integrated into the organization's daily operations and strategic planning processes. Regular monitoring, evaluation, and adjustment of fraud prevention measures are necessary to adapt to changing risks and circumstances.

Where

Nonprofit managers should apply fraud prevention efforts across all areas and functions within the organization, including financial management, fundraising, program delivery, and administrative operations. Specific locations or departments, such as finance, fundraising, and program delivery sites, may require heightened attention due to their susceptibility to fraudulent activities.

How

Preventing fraud in nonprofit organizations involves implementing a range of strategies and measures, including:

- Establishing strong internal controls and segregation of duties to prevent and detect fraudulent activities.
- Conducting thorough background checks on employees and vendors to mitigate the risk of insider fraud.

- Providing regular training and awareness programs to educate staff and volunteers about fraud risks and prevention strategies.
- Implementing robust financial management practices, such as regular audits, reconciliations, and transparent reporting.
- Fostering a culture of ethics, integrity, and accountability throughout the organization, led by the board and executive leadership.
- Collaborating with external stakeholders, such as donors, regulators, and auditors, to ensure compliance with regulations and best practices in fraud prevention.

By adopting a proactive and comprehensive approach to fraud prevention, nonprofit organizations can mitigate risks, safeguard their resources, and uphold public trust. This will also enable them to effectively pursue their mission and positively impact their communities.

6.7 A Case Study of The American Medical College to Prevent Fraud

Introduction: The American Medical College, located in Washington, D.C., is a nonprofit organization that administers the Medical College Admissions Test. It represents universities and colleges across the U.S.A. faced a significant challenge when allegations of $5.1 million of fraud committed by an administrative assistant occurred within its financial department. This case study explores how the American Medical College implemented comprehensive fraud prevention measures to address the issue and strengthen its integrity.

Who

The American Medical College's leadership, including the board of directors and executive management, recognized the importance of involving all stakeholders in fraud prevention efforts after the bank alerted them to fraudulent activities. They collaborated with internal staff, external auditors, and legal advisors to implement effective measures and foster a culture of integrity throughout the organization.

Why

The American Medical College understood that preventing fraud was crucial for maintaining public trust, preserving its reputation, and effectively fulfilling its mission. Fraudulent activities committed by one of their employees, who was using fake names to enroll students, could undermine confidence, jeopardize funding opportunities, and ultimately hinder the organization's ability to support college admission in the medical field.

When

The fraud happened over eight years before the bank alerted the organization. The American Medical College initiated its fraud prevention efforts as soon as allegations emerged. However, the organization recognized that fraud prevention should be an ongoing process integrated into its daily operations and strategic planning. Regular monitoring, evaluation, and adjustment of fraud prevention measures were essential to adapt to changing risks and circumstances.

Where

Fraud prevention efforts were targeted across various areas within The American Medical College, including admission processes, financial management, program delivery, and all administrative operations. Specific attention was paid to the period of registration, and the amount paid. and locations, where the risk of fraudulent activities was higher due to the handling of financial transactions and sensitive information.

How

The American Medical College implemented a range of strategies and measures to prevent fraud, including:

- Enhancing internal controls and segregation of duties to prevent fraudulent activities within the finance department.
- Conduct thorough background checks on employees to mitigate the risk of insider fraud.
- Providing regular awareness programs to educate staff about fraud risks and prevention strategies.
- Implementing financial management practices, such as regular audits, reconciliations, and transparent reporting.
- Promoting the culture of ethics, integrity, and accountability through leadership and effective communication.

Collaborating with external stakeholders, such as donors, regulators, and auditors, to ensure compliance with regulations and best practices in fraud prevention.

Outcome

Through proactive fraud prevention efforts, the American Medical College mitigated and prevented fraud of more than $5.1 million. Otherwise, the organization should lose more than this amount.

After the conviction of the fraudster for 46 months in prison, and implementing new management strategies, the organization regained clients' confidence, preserved its reputation, and continued to positively impact the medical college admission processes. The case study serves as a testament to the importance of vigilance, collaboration, and commitment to integrity in nonprofit organizations' fraud prevention efforts. [1]

---

[1] Washington Post. (2013). Prosecutors say Maryland woman embezzled $5.1 million from D.C. nonprofit group. Retrieved from https://www.washingtonpost.com/investigations/.

Chapter 7

Challenges of Detecting and Preventing Fraud

7.1 Introduction

Detecting and preventing fraud poses significant challenges for organizations across various sectors, including nonprofit organizations, corporations, and governmental entities. Fraudulent activities can manifest in a multitude of forms. These multitudes of forms may range from financial misstatements and embezzlement to procurement fraud and bribery. These acts not only result in financial losses but also undermine trust, tarnish reputations, and threaten the stability and sustainability of organizations. In this chapter, we explore the multifaceted challenges that organizations face in detecting and preventing fraud, highlighting the complexity of the issue and the importance of implementing robust anti-fraud measures.

One of the primary challenges in detecting and preventing fraud lies in its elusive and deceptive nature. Fraudsters often employ sophisticated techniques and exploit vulnerabilities within organizations' systems and processes to conceal their activities. They may collude with insiders, manipulate financial records, or exploit gaps in internal controls, making it difficult for organizations to identify fraudulent behavior proactively. Moreover, the covert nature of fraud means that it can persist undetected for extended periods, exacerbating its impact and making efforts to mitigate losses.

Moreover, limited resources in nonprofit organizations with constrained budgets and staffing can make implementing robust fraud detection mechanisms challenging. The lack of dedicated resources for internal controls, audits, and fraud detection technology may leave nonprofit organizations vulnerable to fraudulent activities that go undetected for extended periods. Nonprofit organizations often engage in diverse activities, including fundraising, program delivery, grant management, and administrative functions. The complexity of these operations can obscure fraudulent activities, making it difficult for organizations to identify and prevent irregularities or discrepancies in financial transactions or reporting.

Furthermore, the evolving landscape of technology presents new challenges in fraud detection and prevention. As organizations increasingly rely on digital systems and platforms for their operations, they become susceptible to cyber fraud, data breaches, and other forms of online misconduct. Cybercriminals exploit vulnerabilities in IT infrastructure, phishing scams, and malware attacks to gain unauthorized access to sensitive information, perpetrate financial fraud, or disrupt operations. Detecting and preventing fraud in the digital age requires organizations to adopt advanced cybersecurity measures, leverage data analytics and artificial intelligence, and stay vigilant against emerging cyber threats. [1]

In addition to technological challenges, organizations must contend with human factors that contribute to fraud risk. Employees, vendors, and other stakeholders may succumb to pressures, incentives, or opportunities to engage in fraudulent activities. Weak ethical culture, inadequate training, and ineffective oversight can create an environment conducive to fraud, enabling misconduct to flourish undetected. Addressing these human elements of fraud risk necessitates cultivating a culture of integrity, promoting ethical behavior, and fostering

---
[1] Joel Chagadama, D. B. A., & Luamba, D. S. (2023). Cyberattacks: A Huge Concern for Small Business Sustainability

transparency and accountability throughout the organization.

Detecting and preventing fraud is a complex and multifaceted endeavor that requires organizations to confront numerous challenges, including the deceptive nature of fraud, the evolving landscape of technology, and the human factors contributing to fraud risk. Overcoming these challenges demands a proactive and holistic approach that integrates robust internal controls, advanced technologies, and a culture of integrity and ethical conduct [1]. By addressing these challenges effectively, organizations can enhance their resilience to fraud, safeguard their assets, and preserve stakeholder trust and credibility.

7.2 Challenges of Detecting Fraud

Detecting fraud in nonprofit organizations presents unique challenges that require careful attention and proactive measures to mitigate.[1] While these organizations often operate with limited resources and rely heavily on public trust and goodwill, they are not immune to fraudulent activities. Here are some of the key challenges that nonprofit organizations face when detecting fraud:

---

[1] Hines, A. K. (2024). *Pioneering Nonprofit AI Initiatives: A Guide to Generational Diversity, Ethics, and Collaboration.* A. Kay Publishing, LLC.

Limited Resources: Nonprofit organizations typically operate with constrained budgets and staffing, challenging implementing robust fraud detection mechanisms. The lack of dedicated resources for internal controls, audits, and fraud detection technology may leave nonprofits vulnerable to fraudulent activities that go undetected for extended periods.

Complex Operations: Nonprofit organizations often engage in diverse activities, including fundraising, program delivery, grant management, and administrative functions. The complexity of these operations can obscure fraudulent activities, making it difficult for organizations to identify irregularities or discrepancies in financial transactions or reporting.

Trusting Culture: Nonprofit organizations rely heavily on the trust and collaboration of employees, volunteers, donors, and other stakeholders to fulfill their missions effectively. However, fraudsters who manipulate trust relationships can exploit this trusting culture to perpetrate fraudulent activities without raising suspicion. The inclination to give individuals the benefit of the doubt can hinder organizations' ability to detect fraudulent behavior.

Lack of Expertise: Many nonprofit organizations may lack the expertise or specialized knowledge required to recognize the signs of fraudulent activities. Staff and volunteers may not have the necessary training or experience in fraud detection techniques, forensic accounting, or internal auditing, making it challenging to identify red flags or anomalies indicative of fraud.

Donor Expectations: Donors and funders pressure nonprofit organizations to demonstrate transparency and accountability in their financial management and operations. However, this emphasis on accountability can sometimes lead organizations to focus more on compliance and reporting requirements rather than implementing robust fraud detection measures.

Fear of Reputational Damage: Nonprofit organizations may be reluctant to investigate suspected fraudulent activities due to concerns about potential reputational damage. Public disclosure of fraud allegations or investigations could undermine donors' trust and confidence in the organization, leading to negative publicity and donor attrition.

Addressing these challenges requires nonprofit organizations to adopt a proactive fraud detection and prevention approach. Implementing strong internal controls, conducting regular audits, fostering a culture of integrity and transparency, and providing staff training on fraud awareness are essential steps to mitigate the risk of fraud. By prioritizing fraud detection and prevention efforts, nonprofit organizations can safeguard their resources, protect their reputation, and uphold public trust in their mission and impact.

7.3 Challenges of Preventing Fraud

Preventing fraud in nonprofit organizations presents challenges requiring proactive measures and a commitment to integrity.[1] These challenges stem from the unique nature of nonprofit operations, the trust-based relationships they rely on, and the constraints they face regarding resources and expertise. Here are some key challenges faced by nonprofit organizations in preventing fraud:

Limited Resources: Nonprofit organizations often operate with limited financial resources and staffing, making investing in robust fraud prevention measures challenging. Allocating resources to programs and services may take precedence over investments in internal controls, staff training, and fraud detection technologies.

Complexity of Operations: Nonprofit organizations engage in diverse activities, including fundraising, program delivery, grant management, and administrative functions. The complexity of these

---

[1] Hines, A. K. (2024). *Pioneering Nonprofit AI Initiatives: A Guide to Generational Diversity, Ethics, and Collaboration.* A. Kay Publishing, LLC.

operations can create opportunities for fraudsters to exploit gaps in internal controls and oversight. Preventing fraud requires implementing tailored fraud prevention strategies that address the specific risks associated with each aspect of the organization's operations.

Dependence on Trust-Based Relationships: Nonprofit organizations rely heavily on trust-based relationships with donors, volunteers, beneficiaries, and other stakeholders to fulfill their missions. However, fraudsters who manipulate relationships to gain access to sensitive information or divert resources for personal gain can exploit this reliance on trust. Balancing trust with accountability is essential for preventing fraud without undermining the organization's relationships with its stakeholders.[1]

Lack of Expertise: Many nonprofit organizations may lack the expertise or specialized knowledge to develop and implement effective fraud prevention strategies. Staff and volunteers may not have the necessary training in fraud awareness, internal controls, or risk management, making it difficult to identify and address potential fraud risks proactively.

---

[1] Suleiman, M. (2024). Effective Strategies Leaders Use to Reduce Fraud in the Nigerian Banking Industry.

Compliance vs. Prevention: Nonprofit organizations face pressure from donors, regulators, and other stakeholders to demonstrate compliance with legal and regulatory requirements. However, focusing solely on compliance may divert attention and resources from proactive fraud prevention efforts. Preventing fraud requires a shift in mindset from merely meeting minimum standards of compliance to actively identifying and mitigating fraud risks.

Ethical Dilemmas: Nonprofit organizations may encounter ethical dilemmas when preventing fraud, particularly when investigating suspected misconduct or taking disciplinary action against employees or volunteers. Concerns about damaging reputations, harming relationships, or violating individuals' rights can sometimes deter organizations from taking decisive action to address fraud risks.

Addressing these challenges requires nonprofit organizations to prioritize fraud prevention as an integral part of their operations and organizational culture. Implementing strong internal controls, conducting regular risk assessments, providing staff training on fraud awareness, and fostering a culture of integrity and accountability are essential steps in preventing fraud and safeguarding the organization's mission and resources. By addressing these challenges proactively, nonprofit organizations can enhance their resilience to fraud and maintain the trust and confidence of their stakeholders.

7.4 Chapter Summary

The chapter on detecting and preventing fraud in nonprofit organizations explores the unique challenges and proactive strategies involved in safeguarding these entities from fraudulent activities. It delves into the multifaceted nature of fraud prevention efforts, emphasizing the importance of vigilance, transparency, and accountability in maintaining the trust and integrity of nonprofit organizations.

The chapter begins by outlining the challenges inherent in detecting fraud within nonprofit organizations, including limited resources, complex operations, and the dependence on trust-based relationships. It highlights the impact of these challenges on the organization's ability to identify and address fraudulent activities effectively, underscoring the need for proactive measures to mitigate fraud risks.

Next, the chapter examines the challenges of preventing fraud in nonprofit organizations, focusing on resource constraints, compliance pressures, and ethical dilemmas. It explores how these challenges can impede organizations' efforts to implement robust fraud prevention strategies and foster a culture of integrity and accountability.

The chapter provides actionable insights into detecting and preventing fraud in nonprofit organizations by drawing on real-world examples and best practices. It discusses the importance of implementing strong internal controls, conducting regular risk assessments, and training staff in fraud awareness and prevention techniques. It also emphasizes the role of leadership in fostering a culture of transparency and ethical conduct throughout the organization.

In conclusion, the chapter underscores the importance of detecting and preventing fraud in nonprofit organizations by safeguarding their resources, preserving public trust, and upholding their missions. It calls for a collaborative and proactive approach to fraud prevention involving all stakeholders working together to effectively identify and mitigate fraud risks. By prioritizing fraud prevention efforts and adopting a culture of integrity, nonprofit organizations can enhance their resilience to fraudulent activities and continue to positively impact their communities.

7.5 A Case Study: Detecting and Preventing Fraud in Rainbow Foundation Scholarship

Introduction: The Rainbow Foundation, a nonprofit organization dedicated to providing educational opportunities for underprivileged children, faced a significant challenge when suspicions of fraudulent activities arose within its finance department. This case study examines how the Rainbow Foundation detected and prevented fraud, highlighting the proactive measures and collaborative efforts that strengthened the organization's integrity and continued impact.

Background: The Rainbow Foundation operates multiple programs to support children from low-income families, including after-school tutoring, mentoring, and scholarship programs. With a limited budget and small staff, the organization relies heavily on volunteers and community support to fulfill its mission. However, concerns about financial irregularities surfaced when discrepancies were identified in the organization's financial records during a routine audit.

Challenges: Detecting and preventing fraud in the Rainbow Foundation posed several challenges. Limited resources and staffing constraints made implementing robust internal controls and conducting thorough financial oversight difficult. Additionally, the organization's trusting culture and dependence on volunteers made it susceptible to insider fraud and exploitation of trust-based relationships.

Detecting Fraud: Despite these challenges, the Rainbow Foundation's leadership remained vigilant and proactive in detecting fraudulent activities. Suspicions were raised when inconsistencies were observed in financial reports, including discrepancies in expense reimbursements and unauthorized withdrawals from the organization's bank accounts. Prompt action was taken to investigate these anomalies, including engaging external auditors to conduct a forensic audit and review internal controls.

Preventing Fraud: In response to the forensic audit findings, the Rainbow Foundation implemented a series of preventive measures to strengthen its fraud prevention efforts. These measures included:

Enhancing Internal Controls: The organization revised its financial policies and procedures to strengthen internal controls, including segregating duties, implementing dual authorization for financial transactions, and conducting regular reconciliations.

Staff Training: Employees and volunteers received training on fraud awareness, ethical conduct, and reporting suspicious activities. Clear protocols were established for reporting concerns or suspicions of fraud to the appropriate authorities.

Oversight and Monitoring: The board of directors increased its oversight of the organization's finances by regularly reviewing financial reports and internal audit findings. Management also implemented ongoing monitoring mechanisms to proactively detect and address potential fraud risks.

Outcome: Thanks to Rainbow Foundation for proactive collaboration and efforts to successfully detect and prevent fraud within its organization. This was doable because of the successful anti-fraud and audit process strategy plans. By prioritizing transparency, accountability, and integrity, the organization strengthened public trust, preserved its reputation, and positively impacted the lives of underprivileged children. The case study serves as a testament to the importance of vigilance, collaboration, and proactive measures in detecting and preventing fraud in nonprofit organizations. [1]

---

[1] Blackbaud. (2023). *Rainbow Foundation Scholarship*. Retrieved from https://calvin.academicworks.com/opportunities/24663.

Chapter 8

Advantages of Detecting and Preventing Fraud in Nonprofit Organizations

8.1 Introduction

Fraud is a pervasive threat that can devastate organizations across all sectors, including financial losses, reputational damage, and legal liabilities. In today's complex and interconnected world, preventing and detecting fraud is paramount for organizations seeking to safeguard their assets. Fraud prevention and detection also help protect stakeholders' interests and maintain trust and credibility in the marketplace. This introduction explores the significant advantages of prioritizing fraud prevention and detection efforts within organizations, highlighting the proactive strategies and best practices that can help mitigate fraud risks effectively.

The Advantage of Prevention:

Preventing fraud offers organizations numerous advantages, from minimizing financial losses to preserving reputation and trust. By implementing robust internal controls, policies, and procedures, organizations can create barriers that deter potential fraudsters and mitigate the risk of fraud. Prevention measures such as segregation of duties, employee training on fraud awareness, and regular audits reduce the likelihood of fraud and demonstrate a commitment to ethical conduct and accountability, enhancing stakeholders' confidence in the organization's operations and governance practices.

The Advantage of Detection:

While prevention is crucial, detection plays an equally vital role in mitigating the impact of fraud when it does occur. Detecting fraud early allows organizations to take swift action to minimize losses, investigate the root causes of fraudulent activities, and implement corrective measures to prevent recurrence. Effective detection mechanisms, such as data analytics, forensic accounting, and whistleblower hotlines, enable organizations to identify red flags and suspicious patterns indicative of fraudulent behavior, empowering them to intervene proactively and mitigate the potential damage to their finances, reputation, and trust.

The advantage of preventing and detecting fraud cannot be overstated in today's dynamic and competitive business environment. By prioritizing fraud prevention and detection efforts, organizations can strengthen their resilience to fraud risks, safeguard their assets, and preserve stakeholder trust and credibility. Through proactive measures, robust internal controls, and a culture of integrity and accountability, organizations can gain a significant advantage in mitigating the impact of fraud and positioning themselves for long-term success and sustainability in the marketplace.

8.2 Advantages of Detecting Fraud in Nonprofit Organizations

Detecting fraud in nonprofit organizations offers several significant advantages that contribute to their integrity, effectiveness, and sustainability. Here are some key benefits:

Protecting Donor Trust: Nonprofit organizations rely heavily on the trust and confidence of donors, volunteers, and other stakeholders. Detecting fraud demonstrates the organization's commitment to transparency, accountability, and ethical conduct, thereby preserving donor trust and confidence. Donors are more likely to continue supporting organizations that take proactive measures to prevent and detect fraud, knowing that their contributions are being used responsibly and effectively.

Safeguarding Financial Resources: Fraudulent activities can result in significant financial losses for nonprofit organizations, diverting resources from their intended beneficiaries and mission-related activities. Detecting fraud early allows organizations to minimize financial losses, recover misappropriated funds, and implement corrective measures to prevent further losses. This enables nonprofits to maximize the impact of their resources and fulfill their mission more effectively.

Upholding Reputation and Credibility: Nonprofit organizations rely on their reputation and credibility to attract donors, partners, and supporters. Fraud can tarnish an organization's reputation, damaging its credibility and undermining its ability to achieve its goals. Detecting and addressing fraud promptly helps protect the organization's reputation, demonstrating its commitment to ethical conduct and accountability. Maintaining a positive reputation enhances the organization's credibility and increases its appeal to donors and stakeholders.

Ensuring Regulatory Compliance: Nonprofit organizations are subject to various regulatory requirements and reporting obligations, including financial management, tax compliance, and governance. Detecting fraud helps ensure compliance with regulatory requirements by identifying and addressing violations or irregularities. This reduces the risk of penalties, sanctions, or legal consequences from non-compliance with applicable laws and regulations.

Strengthening Internal Controls: Detecting fraud provides nonprofit organizations with valuable insights into weaknesses or vulnerabilities in their internal controls and processes. Organizations can use this information to improve their internal controls, policies, and procedures to prevent future fraud. By continuously improving their fraud prevention measures, nonprofits can enhance their resilience to fraud risks and protect their resources more effectively.

Detecting fraud in nonprofit organizations is essential for protecting donor trust, safeguarding financial resources, upholding reputation and credibility, ensuring regulatory compliance, and strengthening internal controls. By investing in effective fraud detection mechanisms and promoting a culture of integrity and accountability, nonprofits can mitigate fraud risks and continue to impact their communities positively.

8.3 Advantages of Preventing Fraud in Nonprofit Organizations

Preventing fraud in nonprofit organizations offers numerous advantages that contribute to their long-term sustainability, integrity, and ability to fulfill their missions effectively. Here are several key benefits:

Preserving Donor Trust: Nonprofit organizations rely heavily on the trust and confidence of donors, supporters, and the public. Preventing fraud demonstrates the organization's commitment to transparency, accountability, and ethical conduct, thereby preserving donor trust. Donors are more likely to contribute to organizations with robust fraud prevention measures, knowing their donations will be used responsibly and effectively to support their mission.

Maximizing Resources for Impact: Fraudulent activities divert valuable resources away from the organization's mission-related activities, potentially reducing the impact of its programs and services. By preventing fraud, nonprofit organizations can maximize the effectiveness of their resources, ensuring that funds are allocated efficiently to support their intended beneficiaries and address critical societal needs.

Protecting Reputational Capital: Nonprofit organizations rely on their reputation and credibility to attract donors, volunteers, partners, and beneficiaries. Fraud can damage an organization's reputation, eroding trust and undermining its ability to achieve its goals. Preventing fraud helps protect the organization's reputational capital, safeguarding its credibility and ensuring continued support from stakeholders.

Enhancing Financial Stability: Fraudulent activities can have significant financial implications for nonprofit organizations, resulting in monetary losses, legal expenses, and damage to fundraising efforts. By preventing fraud, organizations can maintain financial stability and avoid the financial setbacks associated with fraud-related losses. This enables nonprofits to allocate resources more effectively toward achieving their mission and long-term sustainability.

Strengthening Governance and Compliance: Preventing fraud requires nonprofit organizations to implement robust governance structures, internal controls, and compliance mechanisms. Organizations can improve their governance practices and ensure compliance with legal and regulatory requirements by promoting a culture of integrity and accountability. This reduces the risk of penalties, sanctions, or legal consequences associated with fraud or non-compliance.

Fostering a Positive Organizational Culture: A focus on fraud prevention promotes a culture of transparency, honesty, and ethical behavior within the organization. Employees and volunteers are more likely to adhere to ethical standards and report suspicious activities when they feel supported and empowered. A positive organizational culture fosters employee morale, engagement, and retention, contributing to the organization's overall success and sustainability.

Preventing fraud in nonprofit organizations is essential for preserving donor trust, maximizing resources for impact, protecting reputational capital, enhancing financial stability, strengthening governance and compliance, and fostering a positive organizational culture. By investing in robust fraud prevention measures and promoting ethical conduct at all levels, nonprofits can mitigate fraud risks and continue to make a meaningful difference in their communities [1].

8.4 Chapter Summary

The chapter on the advantages of preventing and detecting fraud in nonprofit organizations underscores the critical importance of proactive measures and vigilance in safeguarding these entities' integrity, trust, and sustainability. It highlights the numerous advantages nonprofit organizations can gain by prioritizing fraud prevention and detection efforts, emphasizing the positive impact on donor trust, financial stability, reputation, governance, and organizational culture.

Preventing Fraud:

Preventing fraud in nonprofit organizations offers several significant advantages, including preserving donor trust, maximizing resources for impact, protecting reputational capital, enhancing financial stability, strengthening governance and compliance, and fostering a positive organizational culture. By implementing robust internal controls, promoting transparency and accountability, and cultivating a culture of integrity, nonprofits can mitigate fraud risks and ensure that their resources are used effectively to support their mission and beneficiaries.

---
[1] Wheeler, J. (2024). Nonprofit Leadership Strategies for Maintaining Tax-Exempt Status.

Detecting Fraud:

Detecting fraud in nonprofit organizations is equally important. It offers advantages such as preserving donor trust, minimizing financial losses, protecting reputation and credibility, ensuring regulatory compliance, strengthening internal controls, and fostering a culture of transparency and accountability. By investing in effective fraud detection mechanisms, such as data analytics, forensic accounting, and whistleblower hotlines, nonprofits can identify red flags and suspicious activities early, enabling them to take prompt action to mitigate the impact of fraud and prevent recurrence.

Conclusion:

In conclusion, the chapter emphasizes the significant advantages that nonprofit organizations can gain by prioritizing fraud prevention and detection efforts. By adopting a proactive and holistic approach to fraud risk management, nonprofits can protect their resources, preserve donor trust, uphold their reputation, and maintain their commitment to ethical conduct and accountability. Through collaboration, vigilance, and a commitment to integrity, nonprofit organizations can enhance their resilience to fraud risks and continue positively impacting their communities.

8.5 Strengthening Integrity: A Case Study on the Advantage of Preventing and Detecting Fraud

Introduction: The Bright Horizons Foundation, a nonprofit organization dedicated to providing educational opportunities for children in underserved communities, faced a significant challenge when suspicions of fraudulent activities arose within its finance department. This case study explores how the Bright Horizons Foundation leveraged proactive fraud prevention measures and effective detection mechanisms to mitigate fraud risks and safeguard its mission and resources.[1]

Background: The Bright Horizons Foundation operates various programs to support children's educational needs, including scholarships, tutoring, and mentorship initiatives. With a limited budget and small staff, the organization relies heavily on donations and grants to fund its programs. Concerns about financial irregularities emerged when discrepancies were identified in the organization's financial records during a routine audit.

Detecting Fraud: Despite these challenges, the Bright Horizons Foundation remained vigilant in detecting fraudulent activities. Suspicions were raised when anomalies were observed in financial reports, including unauthorized transactions and unexplained

---
[1]Bright Horizons Foundation. (2024). About the foundation. Retrieved from www.brighthorizonsfoundation.org

expenses. Prompt action was taken to investigate these discrepancies, including engaging external auditors to conduct a forensic audit and review internal controls.

Preventing Fraud: In response to the forensic audit findings, the Bright Horizons Foundation implemented proactive measures to prevent future instances of fraud. These measures included:

Strengthening Internal Controls: The organization revised its financial policies and procedures to enhance internal controls, including segregation of duties, dual authorization for financial transactions, and regular reconciliations. Staff was trained on fraud awareness and the importance of reporting suspicious activities.

Implementing Oversight Mechanisms: The board of directors increased its oversight of the organization's finances by regularly reviewing financial reports and internal audit findings. Management established ongoing monitoring mechanisms to detect and address potential fraud risks proactively.

Advantages: The Bright Horizons Foundation's proactive approach to preventing and detecting fraud yielded several significant advantages:

Preserved Donor Trust: The organization preserved donor trust and confidence by demonstrating a commitment to transparency and accountability. Donors continued to support the organization, knowing that their contributions were used responsibly and effectively to support its mission.

Maximized Resources for Impact: Fraud prevention measures enabled the Bright Horizons Foundation to maximize the effectiveness of its resources, ensuring that funds were allocated efficiently to support children's educational needs. This allowed the organization to expand its programs and reach more beneficiaries.

Protected Reputation and Credibility: The organization's proactive stance against fraud protected its reputation and credibility. Stakeholders remained confident in the organization's integrity and supported its mission and initiatives.

Conclusion: Thanks to Bright Horizons Foundation for highlighting the advantages of preventing and detecting fraud. By prioritizing fraud prevention measures and implementing effective detection mechanisms, organizations can preserve donor trust, maximize resources for impact, and protect their reputation and credibility. Through proactive measures and a commitment to integrity, nonprofits can mitigate fraud risks and continue positively impacting their communities.

General Summary

Fraudulent activities within nonprofit organizations pose significant ethical and financial challenges, undermining their mission-driven objectives and eroding public trust. This book explored the complexities of fraud prevention, the responsibility of stakeholders, and strategies to mitigate fraudulent behavior within nonprofit organizations. Fraud in nonprofit organizations encompasses various deceptive practices, including embezzlement, misappropriation of funds, falsification of financial records, and conflicts of interest. Unlike for-profit entities, nonprofits are often perceived as more susceptible to fraud due to their reliance on charitable donations and volunteer-based operations.

Identifying and addressing fraud requires a collective effort from all stakeholders involved in the nonprofit sector. Board members, executives, staff, volunteers, donors, and regulators are crucial in promoting transparency, accountability, and ethical conduct within nonprofit organizations. It is essential for stakeholders to uphold their fiduciary duties, adhere to ethical standards, and actively monitor organizational activities to prevent and detect fraudulent behavior.

Mitigating fraud in nonprofit organizations necessitates implementing robust internal controls, conducting regular audits, and promoting a culture of integrity and accountability. For instance, by establishing strong internal controls, nonprofits should develop and enforce policies and procedures to safeguard assets, prevent conflicts of interest, and ensure compliance with legal and regulatory requirements. This may include segregation of duties, dual authorization for financial transactions, and regular reconciliations of financial records.

Conducting Regular Audits allows independent audits to identify vulnerabilities and detect fraudulent activities within nonprofit organizations. Conducting comprehensive financial audits, operational reviews, and compliance assessments can help mitigate risks and ensure transparency and accountability.

Promoting Ethical Culture implements a culture of transparency, integrity, and ethical conduct among all stakeholders. This involves promoting ethical leadership, providing ethics training and education, and encouraging open communication channels for reporting suspected fraud or misconduct.

Enhancing Oversight and Governance is essential for overseeing organizational activities, managing risks, and holding leadership accountable. Nonprofit boards should exercise due diligence in their oversight responsibilities, including monitoring financial performance, reviewing internal controls, and conducting regular performance evaluations of executive leadership.

Moreover, determining responsibility for fraudulent activities within nonprofit organizations requires a thorough investigation and adherence to legal and ethical standards. When fraud occurs, it is essential to identify the individuals or parties responsible, assess the extent of the damage, and take appropriate disciplinary and corrective actions. This may involve legal proceedings, termination of employment, restitution of misappropriated funds, and implementing corrective measures to prevent future occurrences.

To sum up, combating fraud in nonprofit organizations requires a multifaceted approach that involves proactive prevention, diligent oversight, and ethical leadership. By prioritizing transparency, accountability, and integrity, nonprofits can uphold their mission-driven objectives and maintain the trust and confidence of their stakeholders and the communities they serve.

Reference List

1. Adebiyi, O. O. (2023). Exploring the impact of predictive analytics on accounting and auditing expertise: A Regression analysis of LinkedIn survey data. Available at SSRN 4626506.
2. American Red Cross. (2010). *Haiti Earthquake.* Retrieved from https://www.redcross.org/content/dam/redcross/atg/PDF_s/HaitiEarthquake.
3. Aziz, F. (2023). *Beyond the Ledger: Enhancing Global Sustainability through Data-Driven Accounting Frameworks.* Farooq Aziz.
4. Blackbaud. (2023). *Rainbow Foundation Scholarship.* Retrieved from https://calvin.academicworks.com/opportunities/24663
5. Blye, M. L. (2020). *Reducing the Frequency and Effects of Fraudulent Activities in Community Action Agencies* (Doctoral dissertation, Walden University).
6. Blye, M. L., & Luamba, D. (2021). Fraud in nonprofit organizations: How to mitigate it. *International Journal of Business and Management, 4,* 385-392.
7. Branet, D. S., & Hategan, C. D. (2024). Bibliometric Framing of Research Trends Regarding Public Sector Auditing to Fight Corruption and Prevent Fraud. *Journal of Risk and Financial Management, 17*(3), 94.
8. Bright Horizons Foundation. (2024). About the foundation. Retrieved from www.brighthorizonsfoundation.org

9. Burk, S., & Miner, G. (2023). It's All Analytics, Part III: The Applications of AI, Analytics, and Data Science. CRC Press.
10. Chagadama, J. (2022). *Small Construction Business Owners' Strategies to Reduce Voluntary Employee Turnover* (Doctoral dissertation, Walden University).
11. Cressey's (1953). Other people's money: A study in the social psychology of embezzlement. New York, NY, US: Free Press.
12. Department of Justice (DOJ). (2020). *Charity Founders Sentenced to Prison for Using Non-Profit to Steal from Donors and Cheat on Their Taxes.* Retrieved from https: https://www.justice.gov/usao-sdca/pr/charity-founders-sentenced-prison-using-non-profit.
13. Dhingra, R. (2022). *The Political Economy of Forced Displacement: Local, National, and International Responses* (Doctoral dissertation, Harvard University).
14. Dicke, L. A., & Ott, J. S. (Eds.). (2023). *Understanding nonprofit organizations: Governance, leadership, and management.* Taylor & Francis.
15. Harmony Education Foundation. (2023). *About HEF.* Retrieved from https://www.harmonyed.org/about/about-hef.
16. Hines, A. K. (2024). *Pioneering Nonprofit AI Initiatives: A Guide to Generational Diversity, Ethics, and Collaboration.* A. Kay Publishing, LLC.
17. International Salvation Council. (2023). *Missions and*

18. *goals*. Retrieved from https://intersalvationcouncill.org
19. Joel Chagadama, D. B. A., & Luamba, D. S. (2023). Cyberattacks: A Huge Concern for Small Business Sustainability
20. Kimmel, P.D., Weygandt, J.J., & Kieso, D.E. (2013). *Financial accounting: Tools for Business Decision making* (7th ed.). Danvers, MA: John Wiley & Sons, Inc.
21. Luamba, D. (2019). *Strategies small business owners use to remain sustainable* (Doctoral dissertation, Walden University).
22. Luamba, D. S., Chagadama, J., Blye, M. L., & James, K. C. (2022). The Impacts of Audit Transparency on Increasing Trust in Nonprofit Organizations. *Global Scientific and Academic Research Journal of Economics, Business, and Management, 1*(20), 86-96.
23. Luamba, D., Chagadama, J., Blye, M. L., James, K. C., & Jaman, S. H. (2023). Understanding the Factors of High Employee Turnover in Nonprofit Organizations: A Qualitative Case Study.
24. Luamba, D., Chagadama, J., Blye, M. L., James, K. C., & Jaman, S. H. (2023). Strategies for Ensuring Small Businesses Longevity: A Qualitative Study.
25. Mandal, A., & Amilan, S. (2023). Preventing financial statement fraud in the corporate sector: insights from auditors. Journal of Financial Reporting and Accounting.
26. Madura, J. (2015). *International financial management* (12th ed.). Stamford: CT: Cengage
27. Miller, S. (2022). *Strategies and Internal Control Procedures for Decreasing Fraud in Faith-Based Nonprofit Organizations*. Liberty University

28. Olaoye, G. O. (2024). Explainability and Interpretability in Fraud Detection Models.
29. Peltier-Rivest, D. (2018). The battle against fraud: do reporting mechanisms work? *Journal of Financial Crime*, *25*(3), 784-794.
30. Rafay, A. (Ed.). (2023). *Concepts, Cases, and Regulations in Financial Fraud and Corruption*. IGI Global.
31. Raval, V. (2020). *Corporate governance: a pragmatic guide for auditors, directors, investors, and accountants*. CRC Press.
32. Solomon, A. N., Emmanuel, O. O., Ajibade, D. S., & Emmanuel, D. M. (2023). Assessing the effectiveness of internal control systems on fraud prevention and detection of selected public institutions of Ekiti State, Nigeria. *Asian Journal of Economics, Finance and Management*, 231-244.
33. Suleiman, M. (2024). Effective Strategies Leaders Use to Reduce Fraud in the Nigerian Banking Industry.
34. Stamler, R., Marschdorf, H., & Possamai, M. (2014). *Fraud Prevention and Detection*. Routledge.
35. Turner, P. (2022). *Complementarity in Organizations: Strategy, Leadership, Management, Talent and Engagement in the Fourth Industrial Revolution*. Springer Nature.
36. U.S. Securities and Exchange Commission (SEC). (2003*). HealthSouth Corporation and Richard M. Scrushy.* Retrieved from https://www.sec.gov/litigation/litreleases/lr-18044.
37. Washington Post. (2013). *Prosecutors say Maryland woman embezzled $5.1 million from D.C. nonprofit group.* Retrieved from

https://www.washingtonpost.com/investigations/.
38. Wheeler, J. (2024). Nonprofit Leadership Strategies for Maintaining Tax-Exempt Status.
39. Yadiati, W., & Rezwiandhari, A. (2023). Detecting Fraudulent Financial Reporting In State-Owned Company: Hexagon Theory Approach. *JAK (Jurnal Akuntansi) Kajian Ilmiah Akuntansi, 10*(1), 128-147.

Made in the USA
Columbia, SC
25 February 2025

6092f494-9ffa-47cf-93be-ed09a7a29cd5R03